COINS
in the
SOFA

COINS
in the
SOFA

*A young adult's guide to spending,
saving, and investing wisely*

LARRY R. KIRSCHNER

gatekeeper press

Columbus, Ohio

Coins in the Sofa: A young adult's guide to spending, saving, and investing wisely

Published by Gatekeeper Press
2167 Stringtown Rd, Suite 109
Columbus, OH 43123-2989
www.GatekeeperPress.com

ISBN (paperback): 9781642374155
eISBN: 9781642374162

Printed in the United States of America

Contents

Acknowledgments

THIS BOOK HAS really been a labor of love. Not just for me but for all of the people who have patiently read, re-read and given me guidance.

I would like to thank Coryanne Hicks for her comments and suggestions. Dinah Emmons, your guidance was greatly appreciated and your challenge for me to reorganize many sections of the book was spot on.

All of the brilliant art was done by a young artist who goes by Yohannes Johnson. He took many of my thoughts and turned them into amazing drawings.

Thanks to Pearl for printing, reading and commenting. And my most special thanks to my wife. Denise—you are amazing. I can't count the number of times I asked you to re-read the book from cover to cover. And each time, you seemed to find a new way to approach a section.

What They Don't Teach in School

L ET'S FACE IT, money matters. It impacts nearly every aspect of your life, from where you live to how healthy you eat. Taking the time to understand the basic concepts of money management may be the best investment decision you will ever make. Ask anyone who knows anything about money and they will probably agree: the sooner you understand how finance works, the better off you'll be in the long run.

One thing near the top of the "bad idea list" is writing a book for pre-teens, teenagers, and young adults about finance. At your age, it's hard to think about saving money for a house or being able to retire comfortably. Those things seem so far away. They are certainly less interesting than friends, music, sports and so on. However, while you may have more *interesting* things to think about, there are probably none as *important* as learning about money. Learning about finance is like taking a pass/fail college course. You may not be graded, but it's much better to pass than to fail.

Since I worked in the financial industry for over thirty years, I naively assumed everyone had a basic understanding of finance. It wasn't until I started to have serious financial conversations with my own children that it occurred to me that most of this stuff isn't taught in schools.

Nowadays, young adults with virtually no training in handling credit are bombarded with pre-approved credit cards. You might think this is pretty exciting—you can buy clothes, concert tickets, and high-tech gadgets right now! Have you ever made an impulse purchase, only to later realize that it was a mistake? Credit cards, Amazon, eBay, and iTunes make it easy for us to get all sorts of stuff on a whim.

But, do you know what happens when you can't pay off your credit card bill? One or two innocent clicks on your computer or phone can quickly snowball into a dilemma that will impact you for years. You can easily start falling down a slippery slope that can hurt your chances of getting a job, renting an apartment, or even purchasing a car or home. Read on and you will learn why it's so important to understand the realities of having a credit card.

Over the years, I've seen brilliant people make huge fortunes. Unfortunately, I have also seen some of these same brilliant people make some very poor financial decisions. I don't want you to be one of them. I want you to make smart financial decisions, and ideally get in the habit of doing so early in life.

The other unfortunate thing I've seen falls into the camp of wishful thinking. People squander money away expecting some imaginary figure to intervene. At one time or another, we all hope for a raise, think about inheriting a fortune from a long-lost relative, or even dream of winning the lottery. While there is nothing wrong with hope, I wouldn't spend too much energy on it as a financial game plan.

Why do some adults have so much trouble with their computers and phones? They probably never took the time to learn about technology. I'm guessing you did. You may not understand how to assemble a computer or build a software program, but you do know how to post on Facebook, Snapchat, Twitter and Instagram. Understanding finance is no different.

You don't have to be a financial wizard, but it's important to be somewhat financially literate.

Even if you live with your parents or rely on them for financial support, a basic understanding of money is indispensable. I want you to be informed enough to make smart decisions and remember that *you* are your own best advocate. It's always a good practice to seek advice from paid professionals, family, and friends. But at the end of the day, your money and financial future are *your* responsibility.

Hopefully, this book will give you a solid base of knowledge about finance. I've tried to write in a clear and concise manner, but the finance industry tends to use lots of acronyms and lingo. When I use lingo or an acronym, I define it (often several times). Plus, there is a glossary in the back that you can refer to.

This book begins with coins that you may keep in a jar by your bed. It will prompt you to think about paychecks, car loans, investments and budgets. By the end of the book, you may have more questions than answers. You may be inspired to search for a deeper understanding of finance by researching other books and articles. At a minimum after reading this book, you won't be at a total loss when thinking about how your life is influenced by your financial decisions.

As you read, keep in mind that my perspective comes from a number of personal experiences. First, I was a young adult once, and I still remember how young adults think. Second, I'm a father, so I know a little about the challenges and lack of financial direction that kids are given. Third, being in the banking industry for 30 years, I live in the world of finance, so I know a lot about how money works. So, relax, take a deep breath, and seize this opportunity to learn from a dad and finance geek who wants you to be smarter than your friends in financial matters.

If you are a parent, relative, or friend looking for something worthwhile to give to a young adult, this book will be a lifelong gift. Countless adults admit they wish someone had helped them better understand finance at a young age. An equal number of young adults admit their teachers never touched upon personal finance topics. Hopefully, the information in this book will have a meaningful impact on a young adult in your life.

License to Drive

CAN WE AGREE that we all need some money in order to survive? Some of us need, desire, earn, and spend more money than others, but for all of us, basic life necessities (food, shelter, clothing, transportation) require some form of payment.

Money is a vehicle of exchange. Finance is your license to drive.

We all know what money is—dollars, quarters, nickels and pennies. While we may not need to start with such a basic definition of money, let's agree that money is a vehicle of exchange. If money is a vehicle, *finance* is your license to drive.

Now, I want to take you a step further and talk about the difference between *money* and *finance*.

Understanding this distinction will make a difference in how successfully you manage your money and ultimately your finances. For example, when I talk about my "phone," an image of an iPhone, Samsung, Blackberry, or some other device probably pops into your head. However, your parents might visualize a landline phone, and your grandparents may even envision an old clunker with a rotary dialer. Words like "money" and "finance" can evoke different images as well.

When we refer to money, most of us are thinking about cash. If we decided to commonly accept buttons or tokens in exchange for gas or groceries, we could also define buttons and tokens as money. Since I don't see that happening, let's stay with cash as our definition of money. Also, since a brief stop at an ATM or a bank teller can help us quickly turn our bank balances into cash, let's include debit cards and checking accounts as money as well.

We'll define everything else money-related as finance, which is more about what we do with and how we think about money. In other words, we have idle money in our pocket or checking account. When we decide that money can be moved to a savings account, we have made a *financial* decision to invest those funds. So, I guess you could say that establishing a savings account is the first step toward taking charge of your finances.

If images of cars, plasma TVs, or jewelry pop into your head at the mention of the word money, you are thinking about *spending* money. Starting now, I want you to begin to think about making, saving, and investing money. By taking the time to read this book, you have already begun to better understand money and finance.

Four important financial terms
you should know

Before we dig too deep, I want to make sure you understand some very basic financial concepts and terms:

A borrower

Most of you will be a borrower at some point in your life. A *borrower* is simply someone who receives something, whether money, goods, or other products, with the intent of returning it. In this case, the borrowed element is money.

If you want to buy a car, charge lunch on your credit card, or take out a student loan, you officially become a borrower. We're going to talk about all of these things in more detail throughout this book.

A lender

The opposite of a borrower is a lender. A *lender* provides money, goods or services to someone, with the intent that it will be returned, and then some. In the case of money, this "and then some" is *interest,* which will be defined next. In this case, we are still talking about money.

While we typically think of banks as lenders because they are loaning us money for cars, houses, and other stuff, remember that you, too, can be a lender. When you put money into your checking account, you are effectively lending the bank your money.

If that doesn't make sense now, don't worry, it will. We'll get into the details of how this works later. For now, just focus on the broad concept of what a lender is versus a borrower.

Interest

Interest is perhaps the most critical financial term to understand.

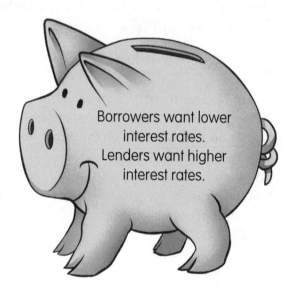

Borrowers want lower interest rates.
Lenders want higher interest rates.

Interest describes how people are compensated for lending money. Said another way, interest is how people are charged for borrowing money.

If you borrow money from a bank, they will charge you interest on that money. Interest is a cost associated with borrowed money. It's usually expressed as an annual percentage, known as the *interest rate.*

Likewise, if you loan $100 to a friend, they should eventually repay you the full amount of the loan ($100) plus an additional percentage of the loan, which would be interest. In this case, interest represents the additional funds that are paid by your friend (the borrower) to you (the lender).

As a lender, you benefit from a high interest rate. However, as a borrow, a lower interest rate is much better. With that in mind, which do you think is typically higher: the interest rate when you borrow money from a bank or the interest rate when the bank borrows money from you?

If you said the interest rate is higher when you borrow money from your bank, you are well on your way to understanding finance. Don't worry if you're confused about how a bank can borrow money from you. We'll get there soon enough.

Term (a.k.a. Maturity)

The final definition that we will discuss in this section is term, also known as maturity. The *term*, or maturity, is the amount of time a borrower has to pay back a lender. Terms can be one day, one year, 30 years, or any time in between.

If you borrow money to buy a car, it's not uncommon for the lender to require you to pay back the loan in 36 months, or 3 years. Thus, the *term* of your loan in this case would be 36 months, or 3 years. Commonly, house loans (mortgages) are structured over 15, 20 or 30-year terms. During this time, you will be paying interest on that loan.

Meet Ben and Maddie

HOW ABOUT WE introduce two people to start illustrating this stuff? Meet Ben and Maddie. Maddie is a saver. She is focused on ways to earn, keep, and grow her money. Ben is a spender. He's always borrowing and spending money that he doesn't have. If Maddie wants a Starbucks coffee, she thinks about how much it will cost and how she will get the funds. Ben wants coffee, so he charges it on his credit card. Throughout this book, we'll see how Ben and Maddie's different financial decisions affect their future wealth, starting with their first jobs.

Beyond the
Lemonade Stand

A s KIDS, BOTH Ben and Maddie did odd jobs such as babysitting and running lemonade stands. During their sophomore year of high school, Ben and Maddie decide to get their first real jobs. They want to have their own money to spend on whatever they like.

They each apply for and receive part-time work at a local smoothie shop after school. It seems like a pretty great deal. They'll earn $12.50 per hour, working 20 hours per week, plus free smoothies whenever they want. They do the math and figure this means they'll have an additional $1,000 per month to use as they please. Pretty great, indeed!

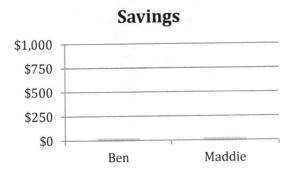

Savings

Neither Ben nor Maddie have had a real job so they don't have any savings yet. But after two weeks of work, they each receive their first paycheck. They eagerly tear open their paycheck envelopes, only to get a rude surprise.

Instead of the $500 they were expecting for two weeks of work, their paychecks are only for $402. What happened to the other $98 they were owed?

Paycheck deductions: Where did all my money go?

Ben and Maddie just learned a lesson we all must face eventually: taxes are a fact of life. That's why you may be in for an unpleasant surprise after opening your first real paycheck. And, it's not a one-time deal either. Taxes will be deducted from all your paychecks!

Most of us earn our first income in cash, from a friend or family member, for baby-sitting, mowing lawns or other odd jobs. This type of income is not normally reported to any federal, state or city government. But, when you get a formal job with a company or start making more money, your income will be reported to the government and taxes will be deducted from your pay.

Generally, when people think about their pay, they are referring to gross pay. *Gross pay* is the total amount a person earns before taxes and other deductions have been taken out. For example, Ben and Maddie's gross pay was $1,000 per month, or $500 every two weeks.

Truth be told, we don't receive our gross pay amount when we work. What we actually receive is called our *net pay*, which is our gross pay minus taxes and other deductions. For Ben and Maddie, this came to a net pay amount of $402 for two weeks of work. The other $98 was taken out to pay their share of state and federal taxes.

Now the secret's out. Math is at the very foundation of finance. Sorry, I didn't tell you this earlier; I was afraid you would stop reading. But I can't keep it from you any longer. If you're ready to go a little deeper, let's take a look at what each of these taxes are and why it's important to pay them.

Federal and State taxes

Tutti Frutti Smoothie
100 Yogurt Lane   Anytown, USA

EMPLOYEE NAME		SSN		EMPLOYEE ID	PAY PEROID		PAY DATE	CHECK #
Madddie Rose		XXX-XX-5512		5431	12/22/2017- 12/31/2017		1/2/18	5551212
Income	**Rate**	**Hours**	**Current Total**					
GROSS WAGES	12.5	40	$ 500.00	**DEDUCTIONS**	**CURRENT PERIOD**		**YEAR-TO-DATE**	
				FED TAX	$ 59.50	$	1,428.00	
				FICA MED TAX	$ 7.25	$	174.00	
				FICA SS TAX	$ 31.00	$	744.00	
YTD GROSS	**YTD DEDUCTIONS**		**YTD NET PAY**	**CURRENT TOTAL**	**CURRENT DEDUCTIONS**		**NET PAY**	
$ 12,000.00	$ 1,602.00		$10,398.00	$ 500.00	$ 59.50	$	440.50	

When you look at the "Deductions" column on your paycheck stub, you can see exactly how much of your gross pay was used for various taxes. The first item under "Deductions" could be federal taxes. This is the amount the federal government's Internal Revenue Service (IRS) deducted (or "withheld") from your gross pay. The exact amount depends on your tax rate.

The *tax rate*, or the percent of your income you pay, varies depending on your situation. The tax rate is based on a formula that considers how much income you make, as well as whether you are married or single.

Since taxes are calculated as a percentage of income, it stands to reason that higher incomes equate to higher taxes. So, as you make more money, your taxes go up as well.

Just when you're getting the hang of this, the government throws you for a loop, but this time it's a good loop and well worth it. It gets tricky, but there are rules that may allow you to lower your taxes. These rules define the use of tax deductions. Don't let the word *deduction* throw you off. We can substitute words like cut, reduction, or decrease and the end result will be the same. Using a tax deduction means that you will pay less taxes than you would otherwise pay without the deduction.

Simply put and considering all other things being equal, would you rather pay $50 in taxes or $100 in taxes? I don't know about you, but I'd rather pay $50. Most likely, so would Ben and Maddie.

As your income goes up, the government allows you to take advantage of certain deductions that can potentially reduce your tax bills.

There's a long list of categories that you are allowed to use to reduce taxes. Some common deductions include:

- The cost of interest associated with a loan on a primary home—very few people have enough money to pay cash for their homes. We will talk about loans later.

- Certain charitable contributions—so the $100 that you gave to animal welfare on GoFundMe me may be used to reduce your tax liability.

- Local income taxes—living in a city or state that has an income tax, such as New York City, where there is both a city and state tax.

- Some "medically necessary" expenses that range from Lasik eye surgery to artificial teeth or hospital care—hopefully, you won't have to ever think about this one.

- Even moving costs can be deductible under certain conditions—perhaps your company wants you to move from Florida to California for your job.

These are only a few examples. Accountants and tax professionals are familiar with the entire list and can help you determine how to fill out your tax forms in the most advantageous manner.

Every year, you are required to file a tax return with the IRS (Internal Revenue Service) no later than April 15th. This return is a government form (called a 1040) that shows how much money you earned and the taxes you paid during the prior calendar year.

Assume your employer withheld Federal taxes of $1,500 from your paycheck during the year. Let's say when you file your form 1040 with the IRS come April, your actual taxes owed come out to $1,550. When you submit the form, the IRS will also expect you to attach a check in the amount of $50 to cover the shortfall ($1,550 owed—$1,500 withheld by your employer).

Had your employer withheld $1,650 in taxes during the year, the IRS would send you a check refunding you the overpayment of $100 ($1,650 withheld—$1,550 owed). As if this isn't enough fun, some cities and states also impose their own income taxes. Some states require you to file annual tax forms with them in addition to what you file for the Federal government.

You can tell your employer how much to withhold from your paycheck using the Federal form W-4. There is a slight bit of pressure to get this form right, because if your employer withholds too little, you'll owe the government money when you file your tax return. If your employer withholds too much, the government will keep more of your money than it should, although they will issue you a refund after reviewing your tax return.

The W-4 form tells your employer how many allowances you want to claim for tax purposes. Think of an allowance as an amount of income that you are allowed to make without paying taxes. A person who only has one allowance will have less non-taxed income than someone who has four allowances. If you are single like Ben and Maddie, you will most likely want to claim only 1 allowance. If you are married and have dependent children, you can claim more allowances. As your allowances increase, the amount of taxes that are withheld by your employer is decreased.

As you make more money and your taxes become more significant and complicated, you may choose to hire an accountant to help you prepare the forms and strategize ways to minimize your tax burden. In some instances, the amount of taxes they save you from paying can offset their fees.

FICA

Beneath the Federal Withholding on your paycheck stub, you will see two other federal deductions known as FICA, or Federal Insurance Contributions Act. Currently, your FICA deductions are 7.65% of your gross pay. These taxes are used to fund Social Security and Medicare. To be precise, currently 1.45% of your gross paycheck is applied to Medicare, and 6.2% goes to Social Security.

Social Security is a program that provides benefits primarily to older people. When you reach a certain age, currently 65, Social Security will begin paying you. Pretty sweet deal! However, there is quite a bit of controversy surrounding this program. So, I strongly suggest you plan for your retirement through your own savings and investments rather than depending on Social Security as your sole source of income when you stop working.

The Medicare portion of your taxes supports a health insurance program provided by the federal government. Like Social Security, Medicare is primarily for older people, too. When you turn 65 years old, you become eligible for the Federal Health Insurance program known as Medicare.

Additional deductions

In addition to federal and state taxes, there are two more deductions you may see on your current or future paychecks:

Health insurance

I'm hoping you are in good health and have yet to see how crazy expensive medical care can be. Did you know that a single visit to an Emergency Room for a broken arm can cost $2,500 without insurance? If you don't have health insurance, an unexpected accident or illness can quickly rob you of all your savings.

Assuming you are younger than 65, you're not yet eligible for Medicare. Therefore, you will need to get health insurance through another provider. When you are working, you often receive health insurance benefits through your employer. The amount of insurance varies by employer. Some companies pay all of your health insurance, while others pay a portion of the premiums. Insurance premiums are another word for the cost of the insurance plan. If you're buying your health insurance through your company's plan, there will also be a deduction on your paycheck for your share of the cost

Retirement contributions

Most importantly, you should be investing for your future. It's never too early to get into the habit of saving. The nice thing about many retirement plans is their tax structure. Some of these plans allow you to defer today's taxes on the portion of your income that you contribute to your retirement. Using these plans will allow your earnings to grow tax deferred. This means that, rather than paying taxes today, you defer them until you are much older and start taking money out of your plan.

For example, if Maddie puts $1,000 into a retirement plan, she will not have to pay taxes on the $1,000 until she withdraws it at a much later date. Hopefully, her $1,000 will have grown considerably before she starts using it.

Not to make things too complex, but there are other forms of retirement plans where you pay taxes today but the withdrawals in the future are tax-free. These types of plans are commonly referred to as Roth IRAs. It's probably a good idea to get some professional help when deciding which retirement planning path to choose.

Why do we pay taxes?

Since you'll be paying taxes, I want you to understand a little about how the money is actually spent. Part of our taxes provide services that benefit millions of people. For example, the government delivers financial assistance when a hurricane, tornado, or earthquake overwhelms a region. We spent more than $135 billion[1] on disaster relief from 2011 to 2013. This money helps cities and counties pay to remove debris, repair roads and bridges, as well as being used for personal assistance in some cases.

Many people depend on government-issued checks for their survival. Currently, around 25% of the government's budget is used to fund Social Security payments to around 40 million people. Additionally, there are millions of people receiving various other forms of benefits and financial assistance from the Government.

---

1   Center for American Progress, Disastrous Spending report April 29, 2013.

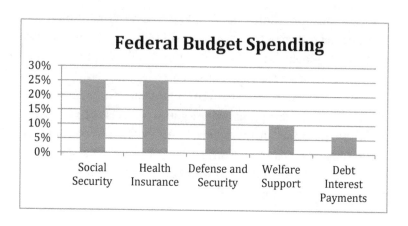

Over time, the way our government spends money changes. At the time of this publication, roughly 25% of the budget is used to fund and subsidize various health insurance programs such as Medicare, Medicaid, the Children's Health Insurance Program and the Affordable Care Act. Just over 15% of the budget is spent on defense and security-related activity. Another 10% is allocated to help families in hardship (low and moderate income working families). Finally, about 6% of the budget is used to pay interest on our country's debt. Yes, a country can owe money just as individuals can!

We will talk more about interest, borrowing, and debt later on, but the United States is the world's largest borrower. Currently, we owe more than $19 trillion dollars to various countries, lenders, and investors here in the United States and around the world.[2]

Few people like paying taxes, but most have come to accept them as the price or cost of living in this country. You can

---

2   U.S. Department of the Treasury, Report on U.S. Portfolio of Foreign Securities, 2016.

learn more about how your tax dollars are spent by visiting the website for the White House: www.whitehouse.gov.

Rest assured there is no shortage of dialogue and debate about fixing, restructuring, and improving our tax system. While the percentages may change, one thing is certain: as long as you live in this country and make money, you will pay taxes, so you might as well get used to it!

Piggy Banks and Pixie Dust

NOW THAT BEN and Maddie have a regular income, they need a place to put their money when they aren't using it. There are lots of good reasons to avoid keeping all of your money in your purse, wallet, shoe, or even hidden around the house. Aside from not being safe, when money is sitting under your mattress or on your dresser, it's not working for you.

Ben decides the best place to put his money is into things. He buys a pair of new Nikes and a new bike and a new pair of headphones and a skateboard and so on and so forth. What little money he doesn't spend between pay periods, he keeps in his desk at home.

Ben believes in fairies. Although he won't admit it, Ben is secretly hoping his savings will magically transform from a few nickels, dimes, and quarters into a lot of money. Of course, this can happen if Ben's magic fairy sprinkles pixie dust on his piggy bank!

Unlike Ben, Maddie does not believe in fairies and pixie dust. She is a saver. She also wants her money to earn more money.

That's right: Money can be used to make more money. We will cover several ways money can be used to generate more money. But before we get too far ahead of ourselves, let's talk about financial service providers.

Phony friends

An entire book could be written about financial service providers. *Service providers* are the companies that determine the interest rates you are charged, the terms of your loan, and the conditions that are imposed upon you when you use their services to borrow or even deposit money.

When we talk about financial service providers, a key thing to remember is that the focus of many of these companies is to make money for themselves. While it may be tempting to think about how nice they are or how much they like you, their friendship may be disingenuous. Don't be naïve by allowing yourself to blindly believe that they are putting your interests ahead of their own. Almost all of these institutions are structured to make money; they are designed *for profit*. In other words, they are not charitable organizations, which are *non-profit*. Therefore, their profit-driven goals may not always be aligned with your desire to make wise financial decisions. While they may not always be acting solely in your best interest, if you are well informed, they can still be helpful to you.

Banks

The most commonly recognized financial services provider is probably your local bank. Most of them, like Bank of America or Wells Fargo, are what's known as commercial banks. At their most basic function, banks hold money (in various forms) and lend money (in various forms).

People and organizations deposit or lend money to banks. When you open a checking account, you are lending your money to the bank. You're allowing the bank to use your money while they hold it for you. It's still your money. You're just loaning it to the bank until you need it. Depending upon the terms of this common transaction, the bank may even pay you a small amount (*interest*) for letting them borrow your money.

If you put money into a checking account, you can get your deposit back by simply writing a check or withdrawing money from an ATM. Under the terms of these types of accounts, the bank must give you access to your funds at any time. The terminology for this type of transaction is called a "*demand deposit*." In other words, you can demand that your deposit be returned at any time with little or no notice. When you use your ATM or debit card, you are essentially demanding that some of the money that you loaned to the bank be returned to you immediately.

Alternatively, you could also deposit (or invest) your funds into a savings account. Once again, the bank is borrowing your money and has an obligation to repay you or give you your money back. Typically, savings accounts are designed to hold funds over longer periods of time than checking accounts. In exchange for letting the bank have your funds for a longer time period and giving up some flexibility when accessing your money, banks will compensate you by paying interest. This is why the interest rates on savings accounts are higher than on checking accounts: the bank is compensating you for letting them hold your money longer and putting restrictions on how frequently you can access your funds.

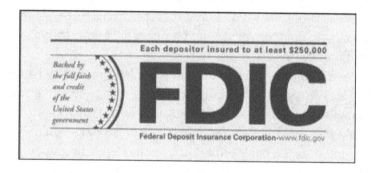

Banks are a popular place for money because they are considered to be very safe. But it hasn't always been this way. You may have studied the Great Depression in school. Before the Great Depression occurred, people did not have a reliable way to verify that their money was safe and secure in their local bank. In order to reestablish trust and confidence in the banking system after the Great Depression, the U.S. Government created the Federal Deposit Insurance Corporation or FDIC.

Today, if a bank fails or goes out of business, your deposits are protected by the U.S. Government. Currently, the Federal Deposit Insurance Corporation (FDIC) insures deposits in banks up to certain amounts (currently $250,000). This means that if the bank holding your deposit goes out of business, the

United States Government will ensure you get your money back, up to $250,000.

Even though banks are widely popular and extremely safe, you always need to be on your toes. One common feature that banks like to offer is called overdraft protection. While the word "protection" sounds good and safe, don't be misled. Overdraft protection allows you to spend more money than you have in your account. If you have $2.00 in your checking account and want a $4.00 cup of coffee from Starbucks, the bank may say, "no problem" by lending you $2.00.

On the surface, that sounds good. You only had $2.00 and the bank was nice enough to loan you $2.00 more so you could enjoy your treat. But the small print allows the bank to charge you a fee for this service. Many banks charge $35.00 for overdraft protection. In effect, your $4.00 coffee could end up costing you $39.00 ($4.00 plus a $35.00 fee). And to make matters even worse, if you order a scone or muffin later in the morning, the bank may tack on another $35.00 fee because you were already overdrawn when you ordered the food.

You may want overdraft protection for an emergency, but using it instead of acting responsibly is a very bad idea.

Banks occasionally offer special promotions in order to attract customers. You need to pay close attention to the specific rules that apply to each account. For example, a bank may offer to give you $100 if you open a checking account. However, in the fine print they may say that unless you keep a certain minimum balance, there will be a monthly charge. As a banker, I have seen many situations where someone's account was eaten up by a series of monthly fees. It is your responsibility to understand how your bank fees will work and what you need to do to avoid incurring them.

Credit unions

In many ways, credit unions function like commercial banks. They are also financial institutions whose primary purpose is to gather deposits and use those deposits to make loans and investments. The main difference between credit unions and banks is that credit unions are designed to be not-for-profit. You have a shared interest and are technically a *member of* the credit union. Credit Unions try to reward their members with higher savings rates and lower loan costs (when compared with banks).

The other difference between banks and credit unions is that FDIC does not protect credit unions. Instead, the National Credit Union Insurance Fund, or NCUSIF, insures most credit unions. If your credit union is NCUSIF insured, your money is insured in much the same way bank deposits are insured by the FDIC. The NCUSIF will also pay you back for up to $250,000.

You may be asking yourself which is better: banks or credit unions? Like so many things, the answer is "it depends." Usually deposit rates are higher and fees are lower at credit unions, but banks may have more locations, products, ATMs and better technology. So, it really depends on what best suits your specific needs.

Check cashing companies and payday lenders

Check cashing companies and payday loan companies operate on an entirely different model. These companies typically lend cash in exchange for repayment from your next paycheck. They can make a cash loan immediately in exchange for a personal check that will not be cashed for a few days, often until your payday. Many people view check cashing and payday loan companies as financial pawnbrokers. These types of lenders loan money to people who tend to be in dire straits. If their situation is

Check cashing companies and payday lenders are often seen as financial pawnshops.

desperate enough, borrowers will agree to unfavorable terms in order to get money. When borrowing money, unfavorable terms mean high interest rates. I want to help you plan so you don't find yourself in a situation where you will need money so badly that you agree to a loan regardless of the terms.

Back to the Banks: How banks make money

After doing some research, Maddie decides to open a checking and saving account with a bank. She will keep money for her everyday purchases in her checking account, where it will be accessible but earn no interest. The rest of her income, she will deposit into a savings account. In exchange for putting her money in a savings account, the bank promises to pay Maddie interest at a rate of 3% per year. This means that after 12 months, if Maddie makes no withdrawals, her $1,000 will now be $1,030. Her money will have made $30 just by sitting in a savings account!

This is a pretty good deal for Maddie. Don't forget to think about another question: what's in it for the bank?

Banks make money by using deposits made by customers (like Maddie) to provide loans to customers (like Ben).

Bank deposits can take many forms. The simplest forms are checking and savings accounts. These types of accounts allow customers like Maddie to quickly convert their deposits into cash. The ease of converting an investment into cash is known as *liquidity*.

If an investment can be quickly converted into cash, it is said to be *highly liquid*. When a longer time period or more restrictions are required before an investment can be converted into cash, it is said to be *less liquid*. Maddie's checking account is more liquid than her savings account because there are no restrictions on how frequently she can withdraw her money.

When someone is willing to forego liquidity, and they can commit to keeping their money invested for a period of time, they are often financially rewarded through higher interest rates. In return, the lender knows the investment will be in place and available to them for a longer time period. This is why Maddie's savings account can earn 3% interest, while her checking account earns zero interest.

The ease of converting an investment into cash is known as liquidity.

When a bank grants a loan to a company or individual, the borrower must agree to repay the loan, along with interest. As mentioned earlier, the amount of interest is determined by an interest rate.

Typically, interest rates that financial institutions charge on loans are higher than the interest rates that are paid on deposits. The differences between these interest rates create revenue for the financial institution.

Let's illustrate this concept with an example:

Assume the bank used Maddie's $1,000 deposit to give a loan to Ben at an interest rate of 10% per year. Also assume that the bank told Ben to pay them back in one year.

The bank will pay Maddie 3% or $30 in interest for letting them hold her money for one year. At the same time, the bank will charge Ben $100 (10% of $1,000 for one year) in interest fees. After collecting $100 from Ben and paying Maddie $30, the bank keeps $70 in profit. Remember what we said earlier about lenders wanting high interest rates and borrowers wanting low interest rates? Clearly, the bank has an incentive to charge as much as possible for loans and pay as little as possible on deposits.

Since revenue comes from the difference between money that is paid on deposits and revenue that is earned on loans, financial institutions have an incentive to attract a lot of low interest rate deposits and make a lot of high interest rate loans. This makes sense, because they're in the banking business to earn a profit. If a bank can make $70 by lending Maddie's $1,000 deposit for a year to another person, imagine how much they can make finding 1,000 pairs of customers? 10,000 pairs? Or even millions of depositors and borrowers!

Introducing risk

One year after opening her bank accounts, Maddie has managed to save $1,000 while Ben has managed to accumulate two pairs of new shoes, a new bike, a new skateboard, the latest iPhone accessories, and a Starbucks addiction. While he enjoys all of these things, what Ben really wants now is a new plasma flat screen TV. Knowing Maddie always has spare change, he approaches her for a loan.

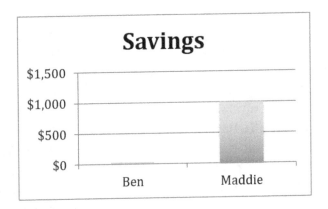

Ben offers to pay Maddie 1% interest if she will lend him $1,000 from her savings to buy his TV.

If you were Maddie, which would you rather do over the next year:

A. Keep your money in your checking account earning 0%,

B. Earn $10 lending your $1,000 to Ben, or

C. Earn $30 by putting $1,000 into your savings account that earns 3%?

The answer, from a financial perspective, is clearly option C. In fact, it is 3 times better ($30 vs. $10) than loaning the money to Ben. However, Ben may not be pleased with her decision.

Her "worst case scenario" is that the bank goes out of business and Maddie cannot get her $1,000 deposit back. Even in this "worst case scenario," she would still be fine thanks to FDIC insurance. Remember, if a bank is unable to repay Maddie's $1,000 deposit, the United States Government (FDIC) will take make sure she is paid.

Always remember that you are your own best advocate. If something sounds too good to be true or someone makes an outrageous promise, beware. More often than not, if something sounds too good to be true, then it probably isn't true. Incidentally, this is a good rule for life and not just finance.

You should always be a bit skeptical with respect to your money. Take the time to understand exactly what is being proposed and, most importantly, what could go wrong. What can go wrong is often called the "worst case scenario." It's easy to only hear what can go right, and sometimes, this is all sales people will tell you. But you should always ask questions and keep asking them until you understand what happens if expectations, projections, and estimates don't happen. The biggest question should be: *What can go wrong?*

Black Magic: Plastic

Credit cards are not free, plastic money

AS THEY CONTINUE on with their new jobs, eventually Ben and Maddie begin getting letters from credit card companies. While some of these letters are presented as once in a lifetime offers, they are essentially advertisements to get Ben and Maddie to buy a product, which in this case, is the credit card.

Credit cards, as most of you know, are little plastic rectangles. They contain magical numbers that allow you to get all sorts of cool stuff.

Sort of.

With a credit card, you can buy virtually anything whenever you want. All you need to do is swipe your credit card and then sign a receipt, or type those magical numbers into an online check-out form. In return, you get a flat screen TV, clothes, food or just about anything else you want.

Does this sound too good to be true? If you said yes, you're right—it is indeed too good to be true.

The problem with a credit card is that you ultimately have to pay for all the stuff you charge on it. One day you will have to send the credit card company money in exchange for the credit that they have extended to you.

If you are able to control yourself, credit cards can actually be a good thing. In fact, in many ways, they are superior to cash. For example, you can keep your cash in an account that is earning interest like Maddie's savings account until you have to make your payment to the credit card company. Some credit cards even incentivize you by giving you points or other rewards to use their card. Some companies offer to insure products that are purchased with their cards. And unlike cash, most of these companies offer some sort of protection if your card is stolen.

As long as you have the money to pay back the credit card company when your bill is due, you're fine. If however, (read slowly, this is important) you can only make the minimum payment each month, you're about to get yourself into serious trouble.

Let's be very clear—if you cannot pay your entire credit card balance in full each month, you are either:

1. spending too much money (in other words, you are making too little money to support your spending), or

2. you have a fundamental misunderstanding of finance.

Let's fix that.

How credit card companies make money

Credit card companies like it when people don't pay their purchases in full each month. That's because the credit card company earns a finance charge (essentially interest) based on the outstanding amount that you still owe. Credit card companies generally charge very high interest rates on these unpaid or outstanding balances. They also earn extra fees from people who don't pay their credit card bills on time.

Let's use Ben as an example. Being an avid spender, Ben took one look at the credit card offer he received and immediately said, "Sign me up!" Now he can finally get that plasma flat screen TV for his room. The TV costs $1,000. Since Ben only has $25 in his desk drawer and Maddie already turned him down for a loan, he was worried that he couldn't afford to buy a new TV. Until now.

As soon as Ben's credit card arrives in the mail, he rushes out to buy his new TV. He charges the new $1,000 TV to his credit card and takes the treasure home in time to watch some football. At the end of the month, he receives a statement from the credit card company showing his $1,000 purchase. It's time to pay for his TV.

Ben looks in his desk drawer and sees he still only has $25. There is no way he can pay off his credit card bill right now.

Luckily for Ben, his credit card statement says it's okay if he can't pay his full balance. All he has to do is make the minimum monthly payment of $25 and the credit card company will let him postpone paying for his TV until next month.

Ben breathes a sigh of relief. He sends the credit card company $25 and forgets all about the $1,000 he still owes. As far as he can tell, the credit card company forgets all about it, too—until the next month when another bill comes.

This time Ben's credit card bill shows an outstanding balance of $990.29. How was that possible? He already paid $25 towards his TV. Shouldn't his balance be $975?

Here is the problem with credit card debt: Ben's credit card charges an annual percentage rate (or APR) of 18%. While this is expressed as an annualized rate, or the amount you would pay for a full year, the credit card company uses this percentage to calculate interest charges on the amounts that you owe *every day*.

Since Ben made only the minimum payment on his credit card of around $25, the credit card company began charging interest on Ben's daily balance using their APR of 18%. This rate is set so that if you continue paying only the minimum payment, your balance will eventually reach $0 (and your credit card will be paid off in full), but it will take you many years to do so and ultimately cost a lot more money than your original purchase.

In Ben's case, if he continues to pay only the minimum balance of $25 each month, it will take him 9 years to get his balance down to $0. And over that time period, he will have paid over $900 in interest or finance charges. After all payments and fees, he will actually spend close to $2,000 for his $1,000 TV that was purchased with his magic credit card.

In this example, the company that sold Ben the TV received $1,000 and the credit card company earned $900. This wasn't a bad deal for the credit card company and the store that sold Ben the TV. But for Ben, it was an awful deal.

Conversely, if you already had $1,000 in the bank and wanted to spend it on a plasma TV, it might not be bad to use a credit card. In fact, the credit card provider may give you points and not require payment for 30 or 45 days after the purchase is made. The credit card company may even offer enhanced insurance or an extended warranty on the TV.

If you let your $1,000 sit in a bank account earning interest for 30 days and then paid the credit card company the $1,000 that you owed them, this credit card purchase would be just fine. It's when you don't have the $1,000, or when you only have $1,000 but buy a better $2,000 plasma TV that credit cards can become dangerous to use.

In summary, if you pay off your entire credit card balance at the end of each month, credit cards can be a fine way to pay for stuff. They can be especially attractive if you get one of those 0% annual interest rate introductory offers. But you should be aware of what happens when that offer ends. After the introductory offer of 0%, interest rates often skyrocket to 12%, 15% or even 20%. If you can only repay part of the balance or make the minimum payment, cut up your cards immediately and stop using them.

Debit cards vs. credit cards

When Maddie opened her checking account, she received a debit card in the mail. While debit and credit cards may look the same from the outside, they function very differently. Unlike a credit card, debit cards do not advance you money to spend. Had Ben tried to buy his TV with a debit card with only $25 in his bank account, he would not have gone home that day with the TV. The bank would have told the cashier at the store that Ben had insufficient funds in his account and the cashier would have declined Ben's purchase.

This is the key difference between credit and debit cards: With credit cards, you can spend more money than you have. With debit cards, you can only spend as much money as you have in the bank. This makes debit cards significantly less risky, but debit cards do not offer points or cash back rewards, nor can you delay paying for your purchase as you can with credit cards.

It should go without saying that you also need to understand fees associated with a debit card. With many of these products and accounts, certain fees may be imposed. Do you remember overdraft protection? If you use your debit card to buy a cup of coffee that costs $4 but you only have $2 in your account, the charge may be approved, but with a fee. Therefore, you may end up owing the financial institution the $2 that wasn't in your account for your $4 purchase, plus you may also be charged an additional $25 fee for the mistake. That $4 cup of coffee just cost you $29.

In addition to interest charges, most financial service providers also impose late fees if payments are not received by a certain date. Fees vary depending on the institution as well as the terms.

Besides costing you extra money, not paying your bills on time can hurt your credit score. A credit score is exactly what it sounds like. It's a way for lenders to assess (or keep score of) someone's credit. These scores are interesting because you may not even be aware they are scoring you.

We all know your high school grades and test scores matter when you're applying for college. Well, your credit scores matter when you're applying for a loan. At some point, you will probably need to borrow money to purchase pricey things like a car or a house. A lender will want to know if you have a good track record of paying your bills before lending you any money. That is why a credit score can have a significant and lasting impact on your life.

What your FICO score says about you

No discussion of credit would be complete without talking about FICO. You have probably heard or seen advertisements about your FICO, also known as your credit score. Now is a good time to think about its meaning.

FICO is actually a company also known as the Fair Isaac Corporation. This company gathers information about you and uses this data to generate an assessment of your credit, which is commonly referred to as your FICO score.

Lenders use your FICO score to help determine the likelihood that you will repay them if they choose to lend you money. Higher FICO scores, also called grades, indicate a higher probability of repayment. If you have a higher probability of repayment, the interest rate (used to charge you for a loan) will be lower.

On the other hand, if you have a low FICO score, lenders will charge you higher interest rates to borrow money. This is so they can be compensated for the higher risk associated with lending money to a low FICO score customer. Remember, higher risk leads to higher rewards—in this case, for the lender.

Do you understand why you want a high FICO score? If you need to borrow money, you want to pay the lowest rate possible. This means you will need to earn and maintain a high FICO score. Low FICO scores make it very difficult to obtain favorable interest rates. To see this, we can again use Ben and Maddie as an example.

Higher risk means higher interest rates

Let's assume Ben approaches Maddie for another loan, this time to help him pay off his mounting credit card debt. She is still depositing her money with a bank and earning a return of 3%.

If Maddie takes her money out of the bank and loans it to Ben without charging him any interest, then Maddie is essentially giving up her 3% return in order to help Ben.

Additionally, while deposited in the bank, Maddie's money is safe and secure. There is an extremely high likelihood that the bank is going to repay Maddie her money—and if, for some reason, the bank can't, thanks to FDIC, the U.S. Government will. Does the same likelihood exist that Ben would repay his debt to Maddie?

I would argue the answer is definitely no. Ben is not as financially stable as a bank. Nor will the FDIC insure Ben's obligations to repay Maddie. Lending her money to Ben would subject Maddie to more risk than just leaving her money in a bank. As a result of this increased risk, Maddie should charge Ben a higher interest rate than she is currently receiving from the bank in order to be compensated for accepting the risk that Ben will not pay her back.

If Ben is responsible and highly likely to repay Maddie, maybe the interest rate should be 5%, or only 2% higher than the bank is already paying Maddie. However, if Ben is highly *unlikely* to repay his debt, 10%, 20%, or even 30% may be a more appropriate rate of interest.

Put yourself in Maddie's shoes. If you had $1,000 in the bank earning 3% interest, and a friend asked you to take the money out of the bank and lend it to them at 0% interest—in other words for free—would you do it?

Alternatively, if you have money and want to loan it to your friends, do you want them to have a high FICO score or a low one?

Ah, but this is a bit of a trick question. If you are most interested in being repaid, you'll want your friend to have a high FICO score. On the other hand, if you are a risk-taker and you're willing to lose all or part of your loan (by having your friend not repay you), then you may not care if your friend has a low FICO score because that means you can charge him a higher interest rate. In this case, if your friend does repay you, you will have earned a lot more than if you had loaned your money to a more reliable friend at a lower rate of interest.

Just remember: When making a risky loan, you have increased the odds that you might lose your money if the borrower does not repay you. Higher risk equals higher *potential* return, not higher guaranteed return.

Not only is it ethical to keep your credit strong and your FICO score high, it will actually save you money through lower interest rate charges when you need to borrow money.

FICO scores are important in other ways. If you are trying to rent an apartment, your potential landlord will want to know if you're going to pay rent on time, so they may check your FICO score. If it's very low, they may decide not to rent to you. Future employers might want to know if you are a financially responsible hire, so they may want to look at your FICO score. Auto dealers will want to know if you're going to pay for the car you're trying to buy, so they are interested in your FICO scores as well. In all these instances, it's beneficial to have a high FICO score.

Buying Your First Car

NOW THAT HE has his plasma TV (even if he is still paying it off), Ben has set his sights on another new purchase: his first car. He still has no savings because all his money is going toward his credit card payments and other spontaneous purchases. He knows Maddie won't loan him the money he needs (because Maddie is too financially savvy to enter into a risky deal), so he decides to try getting a loan from a bank.

Understanding how an auto loan works

Ben approaches two finance companies for a loan to buy his first car. Let's assume finance company A will lend Ben $10,000 at an interest rate of 7%. If the loan was to be repaid in full at the end of 5 years, Ben would pay $1,880 in interest over the life of this loan (plus, of course, he needs to repay the $10,000 loan).

Now assume finance company B will lend Ben $10,000 at an interest rate of 14% for 2.5 years. In this example, Ben will be paying a bit more in interest ($1,910) but it is over a shorter time period. Should Ben care which financing company he chooses?

I'm going to say yes.

Let me help you think about the comparison this way: assume I owe you $100 and I offer to pay you back today or I offer to pay you back in one year. Which do you choose?

Today is the smart answer. Once you have the money in your hand, you can earn interest on it or make an investment with it. If you're not going to receive the payment for one year, you can't earn interest or invest it until I pay you back. For that whole year, your money is earning nothing.

If Ben chooses financing company A, his monthly car payment will be around $198 for 5 years or a total payment (including interest) of just over $11,880. However, if he chooses financing company B, his monthly payment will be around $397 but only for 30 months or a total payment of just under $11,910.

So, if Ben is going to pay around $11,900 in total principal and interest, he'd probably rather pay it over 5 years rather than paying it over 2.5 years, especially if he's on a fixed income.

However, had both company A and company B offered the same interest rate of 7%, then Ben's total payment by choosing company B would have declined to $10,929. In that case, if he could afford the higher monthly payments, company B may be a better choice.

When a finance company makes a loan to Ben for his car, they keep the car's title as collateral. In other words, if Ben can't or doesn't make his monthly car payments, the finance company will repossess the car and sell it in order to get their money back. This means that even though Ben purchased the car and called it his, it was only his as long as he kept the payments current.

If the lender has to repossess the car and sell it in order to get their money back, think about how Ben's credit (FICO score) will be impacted. The lender is going to report that Ben did not make his car payments on time and they had to sell the car in order to get repaid. Ben's FICO score will receive a ding or negative mark. He may have already been impacted if he missed any of his payments for the flat screen TV that he charged on his credit card.

Leasing a vehicle

Leasing is similar to renting. Just as you can buy or rent a home, the same holds true for a car.

When you purchase a car, either you pay for it in full or you take out a loan. Either way, when you finish paying for it, it's yours; you own it.

When you lease or rent a car, you pay to use it for a set period of time. You don't own it. A car rental is usually pretty short term. You might rent a car when you fly to another city and need something to drive for a few days or a few weeks. Leasing, on the other hand, is longer-term, often two or three years.

Had Ben leased a car, he would have given the dealer, or lessor, a down payment and then made payments to the lessor. The lessor would still own the car, but they would be allowing Ben to use it in exchange for receiving regular payments. At the end of the term, Ben would give the car back to the lessor and stop making payments. If he failed to make the monthly payment while driving the car, he would have a big problem, just like if he didn't pay the lender when he bought a car.

Typically, a car lease includes a specific number of miles you are permitted to drive the car each year. If you exceed that limit, you'll be charged a fee for all the miles beyond the limit. You need to be aware of excess mileage charges on a lease before signing an agreement. They can range from fifteen cents to thirty cents a mile. If you have a 3-year lease with 12,000 miles allowed per year, that's 36,000 miles over the term of the lease, which means you can drive 1,000 miles per month without racking up extra charges. What happens if you turn the car in at the end of the three years with 45,000 miles instead of the 36,000?

That's 9,000 extra miles. If the lease calls for a .15 cent per excess mile, you will now have to pay the leasing company or lessor an additional $1,350 because you drove more miles than the lease allowed.

You can learn even more about leasing booby-traps at Bankrate.com.

One reason many people choose leasing over buying is because payments are thought to be lower on a lease than they are on a loan. However, in exchange for lower payments, you forfeit ownership. Hence, you can't sell your car at the end of the lease and get value out of it. There can also be tax advantages to leasing under certain circumstances.

Should you buy a new or used car?

Negotiating a deal is the final step. Should you buy or lease a car from an authorized dealer, a used car lot, a friend, or off the Internet? There are plenty of pros and cons for each of these scenarios, including warranty, price, and trustworthiness. There are a LOT of disreputable sellers in this business. Do your homework.

If you decide to buy a car outright, you'll have to weigh the pros and cons of buying a new vehicle versus a used vehicle. A used car is often cheaper than a new car, but it may come with other issues. For instance, a car that is old may require a lot of repairs and maintenance, which in some cases can be far costlier than the car is worth.

There are many factors to consider when deciding which used car to buy. A car that's one or two years old and has relatively low mileage can be a cost-effective option. Don't be tempted to buy a really cool car that's very old and has high mileage just because the price is more affordable. There's a good reason that cars with higher mileage tend to be less expensive: higher mileage means more wear and tear on the car, which ultimately means more costs associated with repairs and maintenance.

There are plenty of resources on the Internet, such as the *NADA Used Car Guide*, *Kelly's Blue Book* and *Carfax*, which offer insights to help you make a wise choice. You can also arrange for a local mechanic to inspect a used vehicle before you purchase it. There is a big risk in buying a car at a price that is discounted to account for known problems that will need to be repaired.

Safety is yet another important consideration in car buying. Safety features advance so quickly that older cars may not provide the same protection as newer ones in the event of an accident. Insurance companies know this and often provide discounts for various safety features. As a result, your insurance costs may be more expensive on older cars.

Speaking of insurance, another thing to consider before purchasing a car is the cost of your insurance. When it comes to insurance costs, there are a number of things to consider before purchasing a car.

The real cost of owning a car: insurance and depreciation

In most states, automobile insurance is required by law to drive a car. To obtain car insurance, you will have to sign a contract with an insurance company that is licensed to provide coverage in your state.

Insurance companies fall under the broad category of financial services providers. Another way to think about insurance is as financial protection. Insurance can take many forms but let's limit our discussion to three types: automobile insurance, renters' insurance, and life insurance.

When you purchase auto insurance, you pay the insurance company monthly, quarterly or with annual premiums. In return, the insurance company pays to repair or replace your car if it is damaged or if you are in a car accident.

Liability auto insurance helps compensate other drivers for damage that may have been caused by your actions. For example, assume you ran a red light, which caused your car to crash into another person's car. Your liability insurance would pay for their car to be repaired. On the other hand, if *they* caused the accident, their insurance company would pay to repair your car.

Any guesses as to what would happen to the cost of insurance for the person who caused the accident? If you're in a crash that is your fault, the insurance company will raise your insurance rates. In other words, the monthly or quarterly payment for the insurance premiums will increase. If you are deemed too risky for the insurance company, they may even cancel your coverage and refuse to sell you insurance.

If you happen to be a terrible driver, with tickets or accidents on your record, you can expect to pay more for insurance. On the other hand, if you take a driver's education course and are responsible, the insurance company will in all likelihood acknowledge your efforts by charging you lower premiums. Taking a course can be an especially good option if you receive your first offense on your driving record.

Although there may be many factors that go into the cost of auto insurance, you should be aware of your deductible. An insurance deductible is the amount that you pay before the insurance company steps in. Essentially, a deductible is a buffer that you must meet on each insurance claim. Higher deductibles mean that you are assuming more risk. Therefore, a high deductible will mean lower risk to the insurance company. Lower risk to them should result in lower premium payments.

Setting the precise amount of your deductible is something that you should discuss with your agents. They can help you determine the cost of insurance premiums given a few deductible options.

Higher priced cars might have higher insurance rates because the cost to repair or replace them may be higher. You'll want to check all of these things out before making a final decision.

Although we've been talking about cars, let's stay on the insurance topic a bit longer because it's an important topic. I want to briefly introduce you to renter's insurance. As you rent your apartment or house, you may want to think about insuring your stuff. In fact, some landlords even require their tenants or renters to buy this type of protection. Like other forms of insurance, you pay a monthly, quarterly, or annual premium to the insurance company. If your stuff gets damaged due to a fire, theft, or vandalism, the insurance company will reimburse you for your loss.

It's important that you understand the fine print on the policy because all policies are not exactly the same. Like auto insurance, renter's insurance also has a deductible amount. If a policy has a $100 deductible clause, then you would pay the first $100 on a claim. Assume your furniture was ruined because the fire sprinkler went off, and then assume it was insured for $1,000 with a $500 deductible. In this instance, the insurance company would only give you $500 ($1,000 minus $500 deductible).

This is important to understand because a policy with a higher deductible can offer a lower premium or cost. You should absolutely get a couple of prices before buying any insurance. But make sure you're comparing apples to apples.

If one policy is considerably less expensive than another, check the amount of coverage as well as the deductible to make sure you're comparing similar policies. Don't be bashful about asking the agent or company to give you other options. You may want to see the price of a higher deductible with a lower premium, or vice versa.

Another common form of insurance is life insurance. Life insurance operates in much the same way as auto insurance. In exchange for monthly, quarterly, or annual payments, called premiums, the insurance company stands ready to provide a benefit, or payment, to your family if you die. As you might imagine, the costs or premiums that you pay to get life insurance varies depending on a number of factors. For instance, if you are young and healthy, your costs will be lower than someone who is older.

Insurance providers use quite a bit of statistical data to calculate the timing and even the probability of events they insure against (e.g., a car accident or the insured's death). Moreover, they use statistics to validate how often they will be required to pay the benefit that has been promised.

While most of us need some basic insurance (and some, like auto insurance, may be required by law), remember that these companies are writing policies to make money. They're not necessarily looking out for your best interest. Typically, insurance sales people or agents are also compensated on commissions that are earned by selling these policies. This means that they may have an incentive to sell you the insurance policy that brings them the highest commission. This policy may or may not be the most cost-effective policy for you. It might be a good idea to speak with several insurance agents in order to get a few perspectives before making decisions about which policies are right for you.

Car Value Depreciation – 5 Years
Initial Cost: $30,000

Year 1: value declines by 25% or $7,500
Year 2: value declines by 20% or $6,000
Year 3: value declines by 15% or $4,500
Year 4: value declines by 5% or $1,500
Year 5: value declines by 5% or $1,500

CAR'S VALUE IN YEAR 5 IS AROUND $9,000

Depreciating assets

Assets are things that you own. Your clothes, computers and phones are all assets, that, at least in theory, you could sell and turn into cash.

Cars, like so many other things, are depreciating assets. *Depreciating assets* are assets that begin to lose value from the second you purchase them. Think about it: Could you sell your old tennis shoes for the same price you bought them for when they were new? Probably not.

This is because your tennis shoes are a depreciating asset. Used tennis shoes are not worth as much as they were when they were new. The same holds true for cars.

The moment you drive off a car lot, your vehicle's value declines. If you buy a new car, the rate of depreciation is much faster than the rate of depreciation for a used car. The reason for this is that a car loses its value the fastest in the first few years of ownership. Typically, as a car ages, the rate at which the value declines will slow down. A car's rate of depreciation is a good argument for buying a used car, because you're able to buy it after the sharpest decline in value has already occurred.

There are always exceptions to this concept. Maybe a pair of shoes that were worn by Michael Jordan could increase in value like a car that's destined to become a classic. In general terms though, clothes, cars, electronics and computers are examples of things that depreciate in value.

I'm not suggesting that you should never purchase things that depreciate in value. It's just that when you know that the value of something is going to erode, you should think carefully before buying.

Appreciating assets are the opposite of depreciating assets. In financial terms, *appreciation* means, "to rise in value." The concepts of appreciation and depreciation are extremely important when considering financial decisions.

Whenever we are buying assets, appreciation is a good thing. This means our assets are increasing in value. You will rarely go wrong in trying to maximize your appreciating assets and minimize your depreciating assets. Investments are typically considered appreciating assets.

You may be wise to separate appreciating assets from fads and crazes. In the 1990s, a lot of people thought they had uncovered a magic financial formula by collecting Beanie Babies. There were stories of people paying thousands of dollars for these stuffed dolls that cost only $5 when they were first sold. In fact, at their peak more than half of all American families owned at least one Beanie Baby according to a USA Weekend poll. Of course, the easy money didn't last. You can now find Beanie Babies at Flea Markets and eBay for a few dollars.

Maybe you decide neither a Beanie Baby nor a car is the best use of your money right now. Let's see what Maddie is doing and take a look at appreciating assets next.

Preparing for College

BEN AND MADDIE are high school seniors now. They've both been accepted to four-year universities and are eager to leave home to begin the process of becoming financially independent adults. Thanks to her years of diligent saving, Maddie is well on her way toward that financial independence.

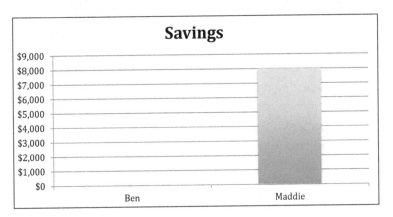

She has continued to work and save at least 15% of her earnings each month. Now that she knows about investing in the stock and bond market, she has diversified her savings from a savings account earning only 3% interest to more potentially lucrative investments. She understands that while stocks and bonds are viewed as liquid, they often work best as long-term investments. Because of this, she doesn't want to use her investments to pay for school. She intends to let them grow as part of her retirement savings.

Ben has continued in his Ben-like ways. He is now the proud (though financially poor) owner of a two-year-old car and a three-year-old flat screen TV, among many other things. He finally managed to pay off the TV, but he will continue making payments toward his car for another three years. At least he learned from the experience with his credit card about the importance of not letting his debts build up. He has begun improving his FICO score by making timely repayments on his car loan. This will come in handy when he, like Maddie, looks for ways to pay for college.

Paying for college: Gifts versus obligations

A college education is important to many people. If a student's family is wealthy, there's likely no problem getting the education paid for. For just about everyone else, obtaining an education and a job-earning degree can not only be a financial challenge, but it has the potential to bury you in debt for decades to come.

According to the College Board, the average cost of tuition and fees for the 2017–2018 school year was more than $34,000 at private colleges and just under $10,000 for public universities.[3] Those numbers don't include the cost of housing, textbooks, transportation, food, computers, tablets, printers, or the myriad other supplies you'll need at school.

As you start planning for school, you should spend as much time researching the various methods of paying for school

---

3   College Board, Trends in Higher Education, 2017-18

as you do the schools you apply to. While student loans are one of the most common sources of funding, there are other alternatives that don't come with as heavy a burden. It is worth your time to consider these avenues before applying for a loan.

FAFSA

All incoming college students should fill out a FAFSA, or Free Application for Federal Student Aid. FAFSA is administered by the U.S. Department of Education, which is responsible for providing over $150 billion in student aid every year.

The U.S. Department of Education uses the FAFSA form to determine your eligibility for federal student aid. They base eligibility on your family's income and assets in relation to your school's tuition cost. Even if you suspect your family's income is too high to qualify for aid, it is still worthwhile to complete a FAFSA.

You can learn more about FAFSA or apply at www.fafsa.ed.gov.

Scholarships and Grants

Unlike student loans, scholarships and grants are not a form of debt. They do not need to be repaid. They may come with conditions you must fulfill, such as participating in particular activities or maintaining a certain GPA, but other than that you have no financial obligation to the scholarship or grant provider.

There are many types of scholarships and grants. Here are a few broad categories of scholarships available to give you an idea:

- Academic achievement scholarships
- Athletic scholarships

- First-in-family scholarships
- Community service scholarships
- Student specific scholarships, such as scholarships for women or men of certain ethnicities

Scholarships and grants are offered through state, government, non-profit and private institutions. There are numerous websites, such as FAFSA, where you can search for scholarships that may be a good fit.

Student Loans

If you have exhausted all other financing options and still need funding for college, it may be time to consider student loans.

Student loans are big business. According to the Federal Reserve, Americans are repaying over $1.5 trillion dollars in student loan debt. There are lots of student loan calculators online. For example: the www.bankrate.com website has one that shows a $25,000 student loan with a 5-year term and an interest rate of 6% would cost you about $480 per month in payments. You would end up paying $4,000 in interest on this type of loan.

Typically, the monthly payments begin 6 months after you graduate. Like any debt, you really need to think long and hard about entering into a student loan. If you are serious about finishing college, a degree will most certainly help your job prospects and ultimately lead to higher earnings. However, if you don't make your student loan payments, your loan goes into default.

This can be very bad. If you allow your debt to go into default, the lender reports this to the credit bureaus which negatively affects your FICO score. The lender may be able to tap into your tax refunds in order to collect on your debt. They may even be able to garnish your wages. This means that your employer will automatically take part of your paycheck and send it to the lender (typically, there are also fees associated— which you pay).

Please be very aware before taking on this type of debt.

Now that you are well versed on loans and debt, it will be much easier to understand how student loans work. You already know that while scholarships or grants do not need to be repaid, loans do. This is why it's very important to make sure you understand exactly what you're agreeing to before accepting a student loan. In other words, you should clearly understand the terms of your loan.

Evaluating student loans: How big is the ball at the end of your chain?

It can be tricky to compare student loans because each one may offer slightly different terms. The key to evaluating them is to understand how each of these terms will affect your monthly payments and overall cost. Let's look at the five main aspects to consider when evaluating any student loan.

Interest rate

By now, you know what interest rates are and how they work, so I won't go into depth on them here. What I will say is that you should carefully evaluate the interest rate on any student loans you consider.

Federal student loans all have a fixed interest rate, making them easy to compare. This rate is set on July 1st of each year. Every recipient of a federal student loan will receive this same interest rate, regardless of his or her credit worthiness or financial situation.

Private student loans, on the other hand, have varying interest rates that depend on the recipient's credit. A borrower with good credit (such as Maddie) would receive a lower interest rate than a borrower with poor credit (like Ben). If you have no credit history or are afraid your credit is too poor to get a fair interest rate, you can add a cosigner to your loan. A cosigner who has higher credit than you may improve your chances of getting approved and at a lower interest rate. Very often cosigners are parents and relatives who are willing to step in financially if the borrower gets into trouble repaying their debt.

Interest rates come in two main flavors: They can either be fixed interest rates or floating interest rates. Fixed interest rates are just like they sound—fixed. In other words, if you invest or borrow at a fixed interest rate of say 5% for 5 years, the rate will be the same each year.

Floating, also called variable, interest rates are a bit more complicated. Typically, the rate will change based on some underlying index. Student loans are often priced with interest rates that fluctuate. For example, a student loan's interest rate may start at an interest rate of 3% but later it may increase to 6% or higher. The interest rates on floating rate loans reset on a predetermined cycle, such as monthly, quarterly or annually. Of course, each time the interest rate changes, so does the monthly repayment.

Repayment options

Different loans offer different repayment options. For instance, federal education loans offer three different repayment options:

- A standard repayment plan of fixed monthly payments for 10 years,

- An extended repayment plan with lower monthly payments for a longer period of 12 to 30 years, or

- A graduated repayment plan where the monthly payments increase every two years.

Private student loans may offer more or less flexible repayment options. It all depends on the specific loan agreement.

Monthly payments

When we talked about loans earlier, we discussed why sometimes you may prefer a loan that you can repay sooner as opposed to one that takes longer to repay. The reverse may be true as well. Sometimes it makes sense to extend your loan term so that your monthly payments are lower.

As a new college grad, it may be hard to find a job that can support a high monthly loan repayment on top of all your other living expenses. Many financial advisers suggest keeping debt repayments at less than 10% of your monthly income.

Do the math before signing a loan agreement: How high a salary would you need to support the level of monthly payments on this loan?

To make life easier, www.finaid.org has a handy student loan payment calculator that not only shows you what your monthly repayments will be given the terms of your loan, but also what type of salary you will need to support those repayments.

Fees

In addition to their interest and monthly payments, some loans may charge another fee to cover the cost of the application. This is sometimes called an origination fee, and it may be added to your monthly cost. Not all student loans will have this fee. Read the fine print carefully to determine if your loan does or does not contain other fees.

Overall loan cost

Once you know all the moving parts of your loan (i.e., the interest rate, repayment schedule, monthly payments, and any additional fees), you can calculate what the total cost of your loan will be. Generally speaking, the faster you pay off your loan, the less the overall cost will be. However, as we just said under the monthly payment section, faster is not always better if you don't have the income to support it. Some loan programs offer loan forgiveness based on your career focus or following a certain number of years of consistent payments. In some instances, if you work full time for a non-profit organization, the federal government or teaching, you may be able to have your student debt forgiven. Please look into this very carefully before making any assumptions or career decisions.

Using Your Money to Make More Money

AFTER DILIGENTLY SAVING 15% of her income for several years and watching it slowly creep up in value at a 3% interest rate, Maddie has begun to wonder if there is a way for her money to grow even faster. She has learned about the difference between appreciating and depreciating assets, and now wonders how she can maximize her appreciating assets to increase her wealth over time. She does some research and learns about *investments*.

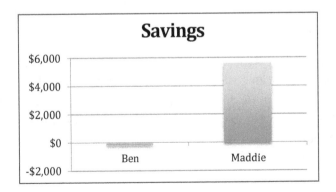

WARNING: proceed with caution

This is important: Never purchase or participate in a financial product until you fully understand the risk involved. Have you ever read about or heard of Bernard Madoff? Thousands of people lost billions of dollars because of this one dishonest man. After the fraud was uncovered, many investors said they never actually understood the financial products they were buying, yet they thought they were investing wisely and making money.

Why would they put their money into something they couldn't understand? Because the sales pitch sounded good. In fact, is sounded too good to be true. Turns out, it *was* too good to be true. (I told you about this!) Madoff was promoting a devastating lie.

If and when you decide to start investing, make sure you fully understand all the implications of the investment you choose. Always ask the question: What is the worst that can happen? Only invest in something if you think you can handle the worst-case scenario.

Investments

There are many types of investments Maddie could make. Let's focus on two categories to start: stocks and bonds. Stocks and bonds can both be appreciating assets. They can theoretically be resold at a later date for more money than you initially paid for them.

We can also think of stocks and bonds in terms of equity (which we haven't talked about yet) and debt (which should sound familiar).

Become a lender: Bonds

A *bond* is like a loan, only you are the lender. The borrower can be a city, state or federal government, or even a company. It's the same idea as a car loan, except for the fact you are essentially the bank. When you lend money through a bond, you will get back your principal plus interest after a set period of time.

Did you ever receive a savings bond as a birthday or holiday gift? If so, you might recall that the bond wasn't actually worth the amount printed on it until a certain date, possibly 20 years down the road. That's because the bond had a set interest rate and date of maturity—just like a loan. It probably cost your gift-giver about half of the face value. In other words, it likely cost $50 to get you that $100 bond.

Now that you understand what a bond is, it's important to

know the term *issuer*. An issuer is the borrower in this case. They issue a bond to the lender. Oh, by the way, I should also tell you that the lender is called a *purchaser*. That's why you will hear people talk about buying bonds. Don't let these terms confuse you. Just know that when you buy a bond, you are lending the issuer money.

At the maturity date (the end of the loan), your savings bond will have accumulated enough interest so the bond is worth the face value. You can then sell your bond. Just as there is a stock market where you can buy and sell stock, there is a bond market where you can buy and sell bonds.

After learning about bonds, Maddie decides to invest $1,000 into a savings bond. She buys a bond that will have a $2,000 value at maturity. As long as she holds the bond until maturity and the issuer of the bond does not go bankrupt, she is guaranteed to get her principal back. Plus, she will have earned $1,000 in interest over the life of her investment.

It's highly likely that Maddie will get paid her principal and interest at the end of 10 years because she did her homework: she checked to see how credit-worthy the issuer was.

There are other forms of bonds that pay interest every year (or every six months), as opposed to saving bonds which pay interest at maturity. Like your FICO score, bond issuers have credit scores to help investors determine how likely the issuer is to repay their debts. The higher a bond's credit rating, the more likely it is to be repaid.

A lower credit rating bond will often provide a higher interest rate to entice investors to purchase it. Remember though, when there is a higher reward there is probably higher risk, too. In this case, a bond issuer with a low credit rating may offer a higher interest rate but there is a greater chance they may not repay you.

Become an owner: Equity

Just like you can own a house or a car, you can also own a company. Well, at least some of it. That's right, you can be a partial owner of Apple, Amazon, Facebook or Netflix by purchasing shares of their stock. Another word for this ownership is *equity*. If you owned some Nike stock, you might say that you have equity in Nike. You might also say exactly how many *shares* you own. A share is a single unit of measurement. It's like the number of pieces of a company that you own.

In order to buy stock in a company, it must be available for the public to buy. When anyone can buy shares of a business, it's called a *public company*. On the other hand, there are private companies, which might be owned by one or two people, or even a small group of people. As long as the owners are not willing to sell ownership to others, it's considered a private company.

When it comes to investments, there are some important differences between stocks and bonds. A bond is essentially a loan, so you know exactly how much money you will get back and on what date. The value of stock generally depends on how well the company and the economy are performing. Unlike a bond, you can hold stock for as long as you like or sell it as soon as you like.

Now that she has purchased a bond, Maddie decides she also wants to invest in stock. Since she's been working for Tutti Frutti Smoothie, the company has expanded tremendously. It now has 800 locations and thousands of employees. Maddie knows the owners personally and believes the company will continue to grow and be very profitable.

Stock in Tutti Frutti Smoothie is currently $10 per share. She wants to invest $1,000 so she buys 100 shares (100 shares × $10 per share = $1,000). After her purchase, Maddie is a partial owner of the smoothie company. She actually owns a very small percentage, though, because a lot of other people own shares, too.

At the end of one year, let's assume the stock's price has risen to $15 per share. Maddie still owns her 10 shares, but they are now worth $1,500 (100 shares × $15 per share = $1,500). If she decides to sell her shares, she would make $500, which is considerably more than she would have earned with that money in her savings or checking account. In this example, she would have been rewarded for taking an ownership position with the smoothie company.

Now let's assume the stock price did *not* go up, but actually dropped to $5 per share over the past year. Ouch! Maddie's investment of $, 1000 is now worth $500 (100 shares x $5 per share = $500). What if Maddie needed her money a year after she invested it?

As an investor, Maddie needs to think about what can go wrong. There's always a chance that a company you invest in does not do well. They could lose money and stop making a profit. A company could even go out of business, which would make the stock worth nothing, total zero.

To complicate matters, just because the company did well is no guarantee that the share price will increase at all. That's because the price of a stock is also influenced by the market.

What is "The Market?"

A *stock market* is where stocks are bought and sold. There are several stock markets where shares of companies are traded. The two most widely recognized markets are the New York Stock Exchange (NYSE) and the National Association of Securities Dealers Automated Quotations (NASDAQ). Outside of the U.S., other markets include the London Stock Exchange and

Paris Bourse, to name a few. So, when people refer to the stock market, they are often referring to the aggregate activity of all these exchanges. Although some markets are centrally located in a physical place, these days a lot of stock market trading occurs online.

To better understand markets and prices, we need to briefly visit the science of *economics*. Economics is concerned with how goods and services are produced, distributed, and consumed. The prices of stocks, bonds, and other financial instruments are heavily influenced by economics. If you have already studied economics, you will grasp these concepts quickly.

If Starbucks charged $100 for a latte, they probably wouldn't sell many cups. Conversely, if they charged a dime or a quarter, their sales would be phenomenal, but they would probably lose money because the cost of making their coffee would be higher than the price for which they were selling it. Finding the ideal price where they will be able to sell coffee *and* make money is tricky. That's one example of economics.

What would happen to Starbuck's if the price of coffee beans went up? Imagine a natural disaster ruined half of the world's coffee plants. Chances are, the demand for coffee and coffee beans would remain the same, but suddenly the supply is much lower. Because it would be harder to get coffee, people would be willing to pay more for it. The farmers who were able to save their coffee plants could now charge a lot more for their product. That means it would cost Starbucks more to make a cup of coffee, and they would probably pass at least some of that cost onto their customers. Your iced caramel macchiato now costs $1 more than it did before! Again, this is economics.

Stock markets are also driven by supply and demand. If there is little or no demand for a company's stock, the price will most likely remain stagnant or even decrease. There will be more people willing to sell that stock than buy it. However, if lots of people want to own stock in a company, the price will increase. As more people are looking to buy, and fewer are willing to sell, there will be higher demand than supply.

In the stock market, prices go up and prices go down. In 2015, one share of Apple stock cost about $130. Three years later, in 2018, the price was over $200. In that same time period, stock in General Electric (GE) went from $28 to $13 per share. Clearly, there is no magic formula for picking a stock, but there are some things you want look at before investing.

First, don't be fooled by the price of a stock. Whether it seems cheap or expensive, any stock can go up or down. The history of the stock price is not always a good indicator either. A stock that has been dropping in price the past year can start increasing just as one that has been increasing can begin to decline. So, how do you know which stocks are a wise investment? Unless you're a psychic, you can't know with certainty how a stock will perform. However, there are ways that you can check the financial "health" of a company.

Public companies are required to issue an annual report about the state of their business, and their plans for the future. I highly recommend that you read this report before investing in a company. It will give you some idea of how well the business is managing their expenses and how they intend to grow their income in years to come. When you're ready to invest, you may also want to look at websites like www.valueline.com and www. morningstar.com. I'm not compensated by these companies nor do I have any partnership or affiliation. I simply like them and trust their research. I'm sure there are plenty of reputable alternatives.

The one piece of investing advice that I will pass along is to beware of hot tips. A hot tip is when someone tells you to purchase a specific stock because they are certain it will increase in value. Aside from being potentially illegal, these types of tips rarely work out. There are plenty of smarter strategies to help you become a successful investor. Take the time to read a book or two and do a bit of homework before entrusting your hard-earned money to hearsay.

If you really want to dive deeper into the stock markets, you may want to start with a few websites. The New York Stock Exchange has a good website at www.nyse.com. The Wall Street Journal site, www.online.wsj.com, can also give you a good overview of current financial events.

I can't encourage you enough to do your homework before investing in stocks or bonds. While there is potential to earn a great return on these investments, there is also the potential to lose money. Remember, when you invest with a bank, your money is insured through the FDIC. There is no such safety blanket with stocks or bonds. If you lose money on one of these investments, it's just gone.

Other types of investments

As we mentioned earlier, there are a lot of different types of investments available. Stocks and bonds are the most common, but you could also invest in things such as commodities or real estate. When you become a more experienced investor, you may even want to invest in the option to buy or sell an investment instead of just the investment itself. Or you could learn to use leverage to increase your potential return on the investments you make. If you're scratching your head wondering what all these things mean, read on.

A *commodity* is something that is a common basic good or product produced in a generic way for sale and distribution. For instance, all refined sugar is the same. At a wholesale or trading level it doesn't really matter who refines the sugar—it all serves the same purpose when used in baking cookies. So, the only thing that entices a buyer to purchase from a seller is price. We are often inclined to buy the least expensive sugar available. Corn, gold, tin, and wheat are other examples of commodities.

Cell phones, cars, and shoes are not commodities because different manufacturers can make different products. Clearly, an iPhone is different from an Android phone and a Ford is different from a Toyota. Like a stock, when you invest in a commodity, you're hoping that the price moves favorably. Back to the coffee bean example—had you purchased coffee beans (as a commodity) instead of Starbucks (as a company) your investment would directly mirror the coffee market. Your investment in Starbucks stock would be impacted by the disaster in the coffee crops but an investment in coffee beans directly would be much more well-defined. When the price of coffee beans increases, your investment in coffee commodities increases proportionally.

Leverage: Using borrowed money

Leverage can be a wonderful concept. In finance, the word *leverage* typically means to use borrowed money or debt to get something you want. You may recall that Ben got into trouble borrowing money. As you peel back the onion of finance, you will begin to understand that there is good debt and bad debt. Ben got into trouble with bad debt. He borrowed money to buy stuff. To make matters worse, the interest rate on the debt was high and the stuff he purchased was hardly an investment.

On the other hand, let's look at how Maddie utilizes debt for a specific investment strategy.

Real Estate Leverage

Leverage can be used in many aspects of finance. For instance, Maddie could use leverage to amplify her returns on her investments (of course doing so will also mean amplifying her risks). To start, let's take the purchase of a home as a perfect example of leverage in action.

Maddie wants to purchase her first home. She is in love with a house that will cost $100,000. She has met with a lender who requires her to have a 5% down payment. If she can come up with the $5,000 down payment, the lender will lend or finance the balance of the purchase price (the remaining $95,000). Maddie has just leveraged her house. This $95,000 loan that the bank gives to Maddie is referred to as a *mortgage*. The bank has lent Maddie $95,000 but they hold the title to her house as collateral. They will continue to hold the title until Maddie pays the entire loan off or sells the house.

Now, let's assume that Maddie makes her monthly payments to the lender and she decides to sell her home after living in it for one year. Also assume her home has increased in value by

10% so she can sell the house for $110,000. (We're going to ignore the fees involved with the sale of a house).

Maddie's return is $110,000 minus $95,000 (the amount she owes the bank), which equals $15,000. After factoring in her $5,000 deposit, Maddie earned $10,000 more than she paid for the house.

You may think this means Maddie earned a 10% return ($10,000 profit/$100,000 purchase price), but in fact, she earned even more. Since she only invested $5,000 to buy the house, she actually made a 200% return ($10,000 profit divided by a $5,000 initial investment).

Had Maddie somehow managed to use $100,000 cash to buy the house and not borrowed any money (or used leverage) she would have only made a 10% return ($10,000 profit divided by $100,000 purchase price). In either case, she made $10,000 but through the use of leverage, Maddie increased her return from 10% to 200%. Not too bad.

The risk of using leverage

When times are good, leverage can be a great tool. However, when things go wrong, using leverage means they can go *really* wrong.

Let's assume that after one year, Maddie had to move. Unfortunately, the house fell in value and now she can only sell it for $90,000. To complete the sale, Maddie must first pay back her loan to the bank, which was $95,000. Since she put down $5,000 to get the loan, and used an additional $5,000 to pay it off, Maddie has lost $10,000.

Remember that it doesn't matter how much you sell your house for, you still owe the bank whatever you borrowed. The bank doesn't share in the profit when the price appreciates and they certainly don't share in the loss if the house depreciates in value.

Another reason you may want to reduce your leverage is to have a lower monthly mortgage payment. Of course, this is only an option if you have enough cash to make a larger down payment. For instance, instead of only putting $5,000 cash into a house and borrowing $95,000, you could put $25,000 down and only borrow $75,000. The monthly payment on a $75,000 mortgage will be lower than if you borrowed $95,000 (assuming all other terms are the same).

Maddie could also use leverage to buy other investments, like stocks or bonds. *Leveraged investing* is the use of borrowed money to buy investments with the hopes of receiving a higher return. However, as we saw with the house, the risk is that Maddie's investments could go down in value and then she'd have to come up with additional money to pay back her loan. Because of this, leveraged investing is considered to be a very high-risk method of investing and not recommended for beginner investors.

When an individual or company is highly leveraged, their returns and their risks could be relatively large. As long as things are working out as planned, leverage can dramatically increase a return. If things take a turn for the worse, the losses could be magnified greatly. Ideally, it's best to use leverage when things are good and reduce leverage when things are bad. In full disclosure, this is much more difficult than it sounds.

Advanced Real Estate

Now, I'm not a property lawyer, and like all other financial transactions, there is a great deal of complexity surrounding real estate. We'll keep it simple and define *real estate* as either land or a building or both. There is residential real estate, where people live, and commercial real estate, where property is used for commercial use (like a store) or to generate revenue (maybe a campground that rents to campers).

Since you are an expert on leverage by now, let's explore how real estate can be so popular. Remember how Maddie used leverage to purchase her home? She can use that same leverage to buy even larger real estate investments. What if Maddie could put up a down payment of $100,000 in cash and borrow $900,000 in order to purchase a $1 million apartment complex or office building that she would rent out to tenants?

Hopefully, the tenants would pay enough rent to cover the monthly payments to the bank. Maddie would still have other payments and expenses related to the building though, like keeping the lawn mowed, repairing things that break, etc. These are called *operating expenses*. If the rent she collects is more than her monthly loan payment and her operating expenses, Maddie may even make a regular profit on her investment.

Income from rents – interest payments to bank – costs of operating apartment complex = Profit to Maddie

+ Monthly Income from Rents
– Monthly Payment to Bank
– Monthly Costs (e.g., trash removal, lawn care, etc.)
_____
= Maddie's Monthly Profit (or Loss)

Then one day, if the price appreciates and Maddie can sell this large investment for $1.5 million, she would realize another $500,000 profit, having only put up $100,000 when she made the initial purchase.

When real estate does well, you can see how people are happy and can make money. On the other hand, a bad real estate market can be very painful.

Global investments

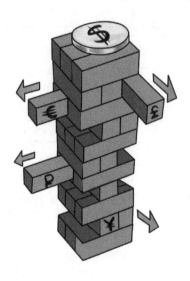

I'm sure you already know that not everyone in the world uses U.S. dollars as their currency. Canadians use the Canadian dollar, Mexicans use the Mexican peso, and so on. Just because a person lives in one country does not mean that their investments are limited to that country. The United States is a part of a huge global economy. Although we are a very important part of the world economy, we are not the only country trying to attract investments.

When an American investor purchases shares of a German car manufacturer that are traded on a German Stock Exchange, the investor buys these shares with euros. (Since the euro is the common currency of Europe, it stands to reason that their financial markets would be denominated in this currency.) If you want to invest in European stocks or Australian real estate, you are going to introduce yet another element of risk into the mix: currency risk.

Currency risk is the risk that the value of the foreign currency you are investing in will go down. For instance, your shares of the German car manufacturer may go up in price by 10%, but if the value of the euro declines by 10% against the U.S. dollar, you will only break even. If the value of the euro declined by more than 10% while the share price only increased by 10%, you would lose money on your investment.

The exchange rate between two currencies fluctuates every second, so when you invest globally you need the share price to perform well *and* the currency to remain stable or perform favorably in order to make money on your investment.

You don't need to be a global financial titan, but I wanted to at least put the concept of global investing out there so you are aware that this represents a huge financial marketplace. Earlier, we identified websites from the New York Stock Exchange (www.nyse.com) and The Wall Street Journal (www.wsj.com). As we shift away from a U.S.-centric focus, you may want to turn to Reuters (www.reuters.com) and The Economist (www.economist.com) for a more global perspective.

The importance of liquidity in investing

Remember earlier when we said that the concept of *liquidity* refers to how easily an investment can be turned into cash, also known as being liquidated? We talked about Maddie loaning or leaving her money in a checking or savings account. Alternatively, Maddie could decide that she doesn't need access to her money for a longer period of time. She could commit to a deposit for a few months or many years with a product called a CD or Certificate of Deposit. A CD is simply an agreement that states Maddie will leave her funds in the bank for an agreed upon time period and the bank will compensate her with interest.

If Maddie buys a Certificate of Deposit instead of leaving money in her savings account, it would still be considered *liquid* because it could be sold, or liquidated, on a moment's notice (albeit with a penalty if the maturity date hadn't been reached yet). Due to the fact that there could be a penalty, the CD is slightly less liquid than her savings or checking account. But this is only a small degree of variance.

Stocks, bonds, commodities, and options are also considered liquid investments. Although they may be worth more or less than what was initially paid for them, they are still considered to be very liquid because of how easily they can be sold.

On the other hand, a house or a car cannot be sold immediately. Ben would need to advertise his car and look for a buyer before he could convert his vehicle back into cash. Similarly, Maddie would likely need to go through a lengthy process to sell her home or apartment building. As a result, investments in cars and real estate are considered to be *illiquid*, or less easily converted to cash.

This is important as you define time horizons by various investment alternatives. If you are investing funds that you will likely need within a short period of time, a house may not be the ideal investment. However, if you're looking at an investment for a 10- or 20-year time frame, an investment in real estate may be the perfect fit.

Once again, be sure you understand exactly what is happening before you invest your money. Always look at the worst-case scenarios.

So many of the concepts that we have learned talk about interest rates. Which leads to the obvious question, what is a "good" interest rate? I'm sure you won't be surprised to hear that there is no simple answer. Read on and we'll dig into interest rates.

What is a "good" interest rate?

Since we now understand that interest rates and yield are similar terms that can be applied to various maturities or time horizons, we can uncover another important piece of the finance puzzle. When we think about interest rates, it's important to put these numbers in some type of context. In other words, is 7% a good interest rate? That's tough to answer without more information.

Are we asking about a 7% yield (return on an investment)? If so, are we referring to a risky or a safe investment? Long-term or short-term?

Or are we referencing a borrowing rate? Is the loan to buy a house, pay a credit card or to purchase a car? Does the loan need to be repaid soon or over a longer period of time?

Can you see how an interest rate is just referencing a number that needs to be put into some type of context? Whether you are trying to borrow money or consider an investment, comparison shopping is always a good idea. It's not uncommon for several institutions to offer similar loans or deposits with substantially different interest rates. It never hurts to compare rates from a couple of providers.

Not all interest rates are created equal

As we think about borrowing money, I want to re-touch on the concept of payday lenders and check cashing services. Often times, these types of companies alter the traditional way that we talk about interest rates.

Traditional financial companies such as banks, credit unions, brokerage firms, and savings and loans institutions typically refer to interest rates in annualized terms. So, when Ben borrows $1,000 at an interest rate of 10% for a one-year term, he will repay $100 in interest.

This is very different from a lender that charges interest by the day or week.

	Traditional Lender	Check Cashing Company
Loan or advance amount	$1,000	$1,000
Maturity	1 year	1 year
Interest rate	10% per year	10% per *week*
Amount of interest	$100 per year	$5,200 per year
Total amount to be repaid	$1,100	$6,200

In essence, a good interest rate is one that properly reflects risk. "Properly" is the key word here. If you are an investor, you want to insure your yield (interest) is commensurate with the risk that you're accepting. On the other hand, if you are a borrower, the same concept holds true in reverse. You want to be sure that the interest rate that you're paying properly reflects your ability to repay (your creditworthiness).

Brokerage Firms: Where you go to buy investments

You often purchase investments through a *brokerage firm.* There are many aspects of financial brokerage, ranging from retail brokerage (selling stocks and bonds to individual investors like Maddie or yourself), to complex global investment banking transactions involving the financial intricacies of large global companies and international governments. For our purposes, we will focus on the retail (or individual investor) side of these businesses.

At times, the lines between brokerage firms and banks can be blurry. Often these companies serve similar or even identical functions. As a general rule, banks take in deposits and use these funds to make loans, while brokerage firms help people and organizations invest their money.

Why you should care about how they make money

Many brokerage firms have an incentive to sell investment products such as stocks and bonds. If you purchase a stock or bond, a brokerage firm will typically charge a commission fee in addition to the purchase price. This commission is one way that these types of firms generate income.

Remember, as the number of trades that you enter into increases, commissions grow proportionately, making more money for the brokerage firms. You need to be aware that there is a cost each time you buy or sell a stock or bond.

You can invest in stocks or bonds as we have already discussed. Or you can have a professional investor manage your money through a fund. With funds, your investment is pooled with investments from other investors and an expert or a team of experts typically manages these investment pools in exchange for fees. As your money grows, so do their fees.

Brokers or financial planners who handle these accounts are often incentivized to manage your money well rather than to simply generate transactions; however, all general rules still apply. Understand the transactions taking place, ask about "hidden" fees, and know what your management fee covers. Always remember, if your investments do not perform well, in many cases, the brokerage firm still earns their management fee, which is an expense to you as the investor.

Budgeting

"A good plan today is better than
a perfect plan tomorrow."[4]

ALL TOO OFTEN, people buy things with little or no idea how they will pay for them. Or, they spend all of their money without anticipating that they may get hit with an unexpected expense, like a car repair or an iPhone replacement. As we saw with Ben, reckless spending can land you in a lot of financial trouble.

Part of being financially responsible is understanding how much money you are making (income) and how much you are spending (expenses). When you know this, you can plan accordingly so you don't spend more than you earn. This is what budgeting is all about. It's simply a plan that you put in place so you know what you can and can't afford to buy when it comes to non-essential items, like fancy dinners or new gadgets.

Over time, you'll need to adjust your budget based on changes to your income or expenses. What's most critical, though, is that you take the first step in creating a budget, even if it is likely to change, and then do your best to follow it.

Creating a monthly budget

Maddie is thinking ahead to when she starts college. She really wants to live in an apartment, but wonders if she can afford it. Being the responsible person, Maddie sits down to draw up a budget for herself. She starts with her anticipated income.

Maddie is lucky enough to have both an allowance and a job. She'll continue to receive $50 per week in allowance or $200 per month. She has been earning $1,000 every month at her job, but she anticipates that she'll need to study a lot more in college than she did in high school. For her budget, Maddie assumes she'll work half as many hours, which means her job is now going to bring in $500 per month.

She can't forget that this $500 is her *gross pay*. She does some math and estimates that after things like taxes are deducted from her paycheck, she will only take home $400 or so. In total, Maddie's allowance and job will equal $600 of income each month.

Easy Budgeting

Description		Monthly
Income: *How much do you make ?*		
Income - "Take home pay"	$	400
Other income (after tax)	$	200
Total income	$	600

Before we start planning for her expenses, recall that Maddie always puts some of her money into savings. She decides that when she starts college, she will put 10% of her income into her savings account, which would be $60 per month.

Note: I hope you can follow Maddie's example. It would be a good practice to begin saving at least 10% per week. The sooner you start a habit of saving, the easier it will be to continue.

Thinking about her expenses, Maddie expects to spend the following amounts each month:

- $350 for rent
- $25 for Starbucks
- $25 for movies
- $50 for dining out and $150 for groceries
- $100 for gas
- $50 for her cell phone

Notice anything odd about Maddie's proposed budget?

Easy Budgeting

Description		Monthly

Income: *How much do you make ?*

Income	Income - "Take home pay"	$	400
	Other income (after tax)	$	200
	Total income	$	600

Expenses: *How much do you spend ?*

Financial Accounts	Student loan payment		
	Credit card payment		
	Savings contribution	$	60
	Subtotal	$	60

Living and Entertainment	Rent/mortgage	$	350
	Utilities (electricity, water, gas)		
	Phone (cell / land line?)	$	50
	Internet / cable TV		
	Home maintenance		
	Insurance (renter's / homeowner's)		
	Movies, etc.	$	25
	Subtotal	$	425

Food	Groceries	$	150
	Dining out	$	50
	Miscellaneous (coffee, etc.)	$	25
	Subtotal	$	225

Transportation	Car payment		
	Gas, parking, tolls, uber, etc.	$	100
	Car insurance / registration		
	Car repairs & maintenance		
	Subtotal	$	100

What's left over ?	**Total income**	$	600
	Total expenses	$	810
	Difference	$	(210)

Her proposed budget won't work. She is going to have to spend less or make more money every month.

Maybe Maddie can get a roommate to split her rent, which would reduce her expenses by $175 (half of $350), and cut $10 from her grocery bill. And she plans to take on another part-time job babysitting or tutoring to generate $50 more in extra income each month.

Turn the page to see Maddie's revised budget after she made a few tweaks.

Easy Budgeting

Description	Monthly

Income: *How much do you make ?*

	Description	Monthly
Income	Income - "Take home pay"	$ 400
	Other income (after tax)	$ 200
	Total income	$ 600

Expenses: *How much do you spend ?*

	Description	Monthly
Financial Accounts	Student loan payment	
	Credit card payment	
	Savings contribution	$ 60
	Subtotal	$ 60

	Description	Monthly
Living and Entertainment	Rent/mortgage	$ 175
	Utilities (electricity, water, gas)	
	Phone (cell / land line?)	$ 50
	Internet / cable TV	
	Home maintenance	
	Insurance (renter's / homeowner's)	
	Movies, etc.	$ 25
	Subtotal	$ 250

	Description	Monthly
Food	Groceries	$ 150
	Dining out	$ 50
	Miscellaneous (coffee, etc.)	$ 25
	Subtotal	$ 225

	Description	Monthly
Transportation	Car payment	
	Gas, parking, tolls, uber, etc.	$ 100
	Car insurance / registration	
	Car repairs & maintenance	
	Subtotal	$ 100

	Description	Monthly
What's left over ?	Total income	$ 650
	Total expenses	$ 635
	Difference	$ 15

An easy way to create your first budget is to keep track of most everything you spend for a week: every soda, every lunch, every Starbucks purchase, and every parking meter. After a week you'll have a pretty good idea of where your money goes— and you'll be surprised at how all those small expenses add up.

You don't have to account for every single penny in your budget, but it is important that you begin to have an idea of where your money comes from and where it goes. Each month, check to see how your actual expenses line up with what you planned for in your budget. This will tell you whether or not you need to adjust your budget.

At the end of this book, I have enclosed a blank template for you to copy and use. Although it says "Monthly," you may decide that a weekly budget works better for you.

Now, let's think about a budget over the long-term.

Creating a long-term budget

Long-Term Budgeting

Description		Monthly	Annual	4 - year plan
Income: *How much do you make ?*				
Income	Income - "Take home pay"	$ 400	$ 4,800.0	$ 19,200.0
	Other income (after tax)	$ 250	$ 3,000.0	$ 12,000.0
	Total income	$ 650	$ 7,800.0	$ 31,200.0
Expenses: *How much do you spend ?*				
Financial Accounts	Student loan payment		$ -	$ -
	Credit card payment		$ -	$ -
	Savings contribution	$ 60	$ 720.0	$ 2,880.0
	Subtotal	$ 60	$ 720.0	$ 2,880.0
Living and Entertainment	Rent/mortgage	$ 175	$ 2,100.0	$ 8,400.0
	Utilities (electricity, water, gas)		$ -	$ -
	Phone (cell / land line?)	$ 50	$ 600.0	$ 2,400.0
	Internet / cable TV		$ -	$ -
	Home maintenance		$ -	$ -
	Insurance (renter's / homeowner's)		$ -	$ -
	Movies, etc.	$ 25	$ 300.0	$ 1,200.0
	Subtotal	$ 250	$ 3,000.0	$ 12,000.0
Food	Groceries	$ 150	$ 1,800.0	$ 7,200.0
	Dining out	$ 25	$ 300.0	$ 1,200.0
	Miscellaneous (coffee, etc.)	$ 25	$ 300.0	$ 1,200.0
	Subtotal	$ 200	$ 2,400.0	$ 9,600.0
Transportation	Car payment		$ -	$ -
	Gas, parking, tolls, uber, etc.	$ 100	$ 1,200.0	$ 4,800.0
	Car insurance / registration		$ -	$ -
	Car repairs & maintenance			
	Subtotal	$ 100	$ 1,200.0	$ 4,800.0
What's left over ?	**Total income**	$ 650	$ 7,800.0	$ 31,200.0
	Total expenses	$ 610	$ 7,320.0	$ 29,280.0
	Difference	$ 40	$ 480.0	$ 1,920.0

Let's say Maddie cuts her Starbucks expense to $20 per week by brewing coffee at home. Next, she cuts her fast food budget in half by eating more meals in her apartment. If she could truly stick to this discipline and put her new savings in the bank, she could save an additional $6.25 per week or $25 per month or $300 per year.

At the end of four years, she would have accumulated over $1,900 from smart planning.

If she puts this money in her bank account, it could also earn interest.

$2,000 Coffee?

Maddie has budgeted $10 per week for Starbucks. Ben, on the other hand, loves to stop by Starbucks every morning. He spends $5 on his drink and tips the pretty cashier another $1.

He rationalizes his Starbucks treat because "it's only $6." But the truth is a bit more complicated. Yes, Ben is only spending $6 per day, but because he stops every day, his coffee bill is adding up to $42 per week or over $2,000 per year. Think about this over the course of 5 years. How much money would he have spent on coffee? Over $10,000!

Ben would be much better off buying a $25 coffee maker and spending $25 dollars each month on beans to make his coffee at home.

The magic of compounding

Here are some crazy numbers for you to think about:

Assume Maddie saves $50 each month by hardly ever dining out and making her coffee at home. She puts her savings in the bank and earns 6.5% interest. Remember, that's the annual interest rate. On a monthly basis, her money earns .54% interest

(6.5% divided by 12 months). After the first month, her $50 would earn $.27, bringing her total to $50.27.

In the second month, she adds another $50. Now her balance is $100.27 and she earns $.54 in interest. The following month, she adds another $50 to her savings and her bank account balance becomes $151.63. After a year, Maddie has accumulated $621.55

> If you can save $200 per month and earn 6.5%% in interest you will have over $1 million in 50 years.

by saving $50 per month. If she continued this habit for 10 years, she would have a total of $8,465.95 in her account.

This concept of adding the interest earnings to the savings is also known as *compounding*, which we talked about in the section on loans.

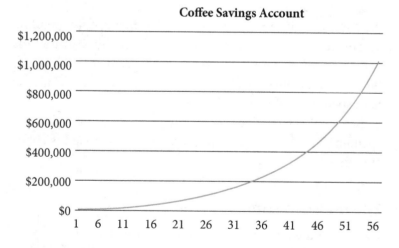

Coffee Savings Account

Now for the magic: If Maddie can find a way to save $120 per month and earn 6.50% in interest, in 720 months (or 60 years) she will have amassed over $1 million. Of course, Ben can do this too.

Not too bad for cutting back on a few Starbucks, eating at home more often, and finding a few other ways to cut expenses.

I realize that it is very difficult for a young adult to plan 60 years into the future. Mainly, you're worried about what you're doing this weekend. But the reality is, the sooner you begin thinking about money, finance, and planning, the better off you will be over the long haul.

Discipline

Some of you may be gifted in certain ways. You may not need to study, yet you're still able to do well in school. Others don't practice much, but easily excel in sports. Still others can eat whatever they please and not have a weight problem. This section is written for those of you who don't have a special gift for finance.

For a lot of people, spending money is a rush. Buying the latest outfit, CD, or gadget can be a thrill. Let's face it, who doesn't like it when someone comes up to you and says, "Wow, where did you get that (fill in the blank)?" You would never expect someone to approach you and say, "Wow, I heard you deposited $25 dollars into your savings account! Way to go." When we seek validation and instant gratification, spending money is often the quickest and easiest way to do that.

Therefore, you need to be your own cheerleader. Establish personal goals. First, try to accumulate $50 in savings. Next, shoot for $100, and so on. Before you know it, you will be thinking about how to invest your savings.

When that time comes, you will already be familiar with terms like: liquidity, investment time horizons, and risk vs. return. You'll be able to think logically about making the decision to buy a Certificate of Deposit (CD) from your local bank or to take an ownership position in the bank by buying shares of the bank's stock. You will understand why you don't want to carry an unpaid credit card balance with a finance charge of 21% when you have money in the bank earning 4%. You can feel in control of your future knowing that you are dialed into your own financial matters.

The Future Awaits: Where Ben and Maddie are now

WHEN THEY GRADUATE from college, Ben and Maddie are in very different financial circumstances. Thanks to her diligent saving, Maddie graduates with nearly $10,000 in savings while Ben still has only the $25 in his desk drawer (what is left over from his last paycheck).

After they get full-time jobs, Maddie continues to save. She puts $4,500 per year toward her retirement. If she keeps this up, by the time she turns 65 years old, she will have saved $180,000 in principal. Since she will also be earning compound interest on her savings, her retirement nest egg will have grown to over $1 million.

Ben eventually catches on to the importance of saving. At 35 years of age, he starts following Maddie's lead and also puts $4,500 per year into his retirement plan. Because of his late start, by the time Ben is 65 years old, he will have only saved $135,000 in principal. Since the funds did not have as long to grow (and compound), Ben will be left with just under $500,000 at his retirement age of 65 years old, or half as much as Maddie has.

Here is a graphic example of the power of compounding

showing how Maddie and Bens' retirement contributions would have grown at a 7% compound interest rate: Maddie only contributed $45,000 more than Ben (due to Ben's late start) but because of the time value of money, she ended up with more than double Ben's savings.

Power of Compounding

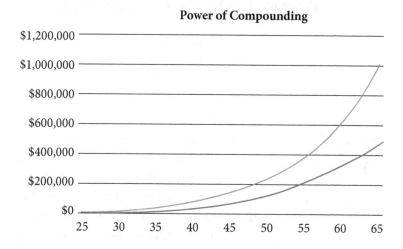

I hope the lesson here is clear: The sooner you start saving, the better. When it comes to savings and investing, time is a good thing.

After reading this, I hope you are not still depending on pixie dust or scrounging around the sofa cushions for your financial future. You now have the tools to start a budget, pay attention to how you spend your money, and begin saving for your future.

In closing, I want you to have three takeaways from this book.

First, taking on credit card debt just to buy things you can't afford usually doesn't end well.

Second, save and invest early while time is on your side. Although it may never be too late, the sooner you start saving and investing the better.

Third, don't be a sucker or allow yourself to be taken advantage of. When it comes to borrowing and investing, ask a lot of questions about fees and risk.

A Word from the Author

To Parents, Grandparents, and Future Parents:

REGARDLESS OF YOUR financial knowledge, I think others can learn from your experiences. I wish someone had shared their financial experiences with me when I was a kid, rather than leaving me to figure things out for myself through trial and error.

Things are so much different now than when we were kids. I suspect you all have fond memories of opening a paycheck, tallying tips, or somehow assessing your money. When you made a purchase, you had to actually part with cash. Well, that has all been lost on younger generations, thanks to things like direct deposits and credit cards. Young adults today rarely use cash. Everything is swiped or paid electronically. I think valuing money is more difficult for the next generation because they don't really see it or touch it.

That said, I would like to share some lessons that I've learned over the years, along with some tips for you when you teach your own kids to be financially responsible adults.

Lesson # 1: Friend vs. Parent

I thought I was being a good parent by buying our children the latest iPhone. Every two years or so one of them lost, broke, or otherwise justified why they needed the latest version, so I bought new ones. In total, I think I bought 6 iPhones and spent around $3,000 over a 10-year period.

Of course, hindsight is 20/20, but I could have used this as an early opportunity to begin teaching my kids about finance. At the same time, I could have invested in my children's future instead of satisfying their technological whims. In other words, what if I had invested in Apple's stock instead of their phones?

It's not unreasonable to assume that $3,000 invested in Apple stock could have turned into $10,000 or $15,000 over a 10-year period. Had I done this, my children would have a healthy investment portfolio today, along with a valuable lesson, as opposed to a handful of worthless old phones. Not a bad gift to help them begin taking control of their own financial futures.

Lesson # 2: Talk openly and often about finance

I thought I was being very clever by taking my son to the bank when he was about six years old. I introduced him to some of my co-workers and opened a $500 savings account in his name. He was thrilled and excited.

Over the next few months, we both forgot about the account. He never saw or touched the balance and over the course of many years, his $500 grew to a whopping $505.

Looking back now, I see that I missed a great opportunity to teach him about investment alternatives and guide him through his first financial decisions. We could have done so much more with that $500 if I'd only had important conversations about saving and investing.

Lesson # 3: Reinforce the habit of savings

When our kids were young, we used to pay them a quarter to eat roasted Brussels sprouts. This was going well for our daughter until her cover was blown. Our son realized that his sister actually liked Brussels sprouts, so he cried foul and the "rewards for healthy eating" program was over.

We rewarded the kids for other things too, like doing extra chores. However, because it seemed to bring them so much joy, we let them spend their reward money on silly things. In hindsight, I should have encouraged them to save their money. Perhaps I could have even rewarded them for saving. It is never too early to get kids started on the concept of saving money.

Lesson # 4: Give your children financial responsibility

Some parents believe in paying children to perform chores. Others believe chores are their children's responsibility in exchange for child rearing. I've learned never to push back or argue about how people raise their kids. However, I think children need to learn sooner rather than later that work equals pay.

Volunteer work aside, how would you feel if your boss asked you to come in early on a weekend to do some unpaid chores around the office? What if he or she told you something like, "This is just the price you have to pay to be a part of this glorious company." I don't know about you, but I think I would be less than thrilled.

Even if you believe children should have certain responsibilities as a way to contribute to the household, I encourage you to find additional things your children can do for pay. I don't think the pay you give your children should break the family's bank. Rather, it is more important to instill the concept of reward for work.

Lesson # 5: He's an adult and I'm still learning.

It's never too late to teach. And, it's never too late to learn. Like so many kids, our children have gotten into their fair share of financial trouble. However, our son recently approached me with his plan to restructure and repay his debts. I was blown away by the thoughtfulness and sophistication of his plans. In all honesty, I didn't fully understand what he was proposing and had to do research to get up to speed.

I loved it—the parent, teacher, and mentor had become the student.

I hope this book will be of help to all of you as teachers, mentors and students.

Glossary

We used a lot of financial lingo in this book. Here is a good key that may be useful.

Appreciation: To appreciate means to increase in value. It is used throughout the book to describe when a stock, bond, or other asset goes up in value. Maddie's house, for example, appreciated in value.

Brokerage firm: A company or institution that facilitates the buying and selling of financial products such as stocks, bonds, and mutual funds.

Compound interest: The process of adding interest that has been earned to the principal balance or reinvesting interest. The effect is that interest is earned on interest.

Credit risk: The risk of default by a borrower. In other words, the probability that the borrower will not pay back what they borrowed.

Debt: Money owed by one party to another. The party owing the debt is referred to as the Debtor. The party who is owed the money is known as the Creditor.

Demand deposit: Money such as a checking account that is held in a financial institution, and can be withdrawn without penalty at any time.

Depreciation: To depreciate is to decline or go down in value. We talked about the decrease in value of an asset such as a car.

Equity: Another word for ownership. If you and several of your friends owned an ice cream shop, you would each have some equity in the business.

Gross pay: Total pay before taxes and other deductions are subtracted from your paycheck. Once these deductions are taken out, the amount left is referred to as net pay.

Income: The sum of all wages, interest, profits, and other forms of earnings received.

Interest rate: The percent of a loan that is charged to the borrower for use of the money. Remember, anyone can lend money and charge interest.

Liquidity: How hard or easy it is use to convert an asset or investment into cash.

Market: A system or place where financial products are bought and sold.

Maturity date: The end date on a loan. This is the date that money or a debt is to be repaid.

Mortgage: A loan that is specifically used for buying real estate. When a mortgage is not repaid according to the terms, the lender can take ownership of the real estate and sell it.

Net pay: The actual amount of money that is available in a paycheck after taxes and other deductions have been taken out.

Obligation: The moral or legal contract that makes one person or party committed to do something. A borrower has an obligation to repay a lender.

Private companies: Companies that are not owned by the public. Private companies are controlled by a small number of owners. Stock or equity ownership in these companies is not offered to outside investors.

Public companies: Ownership in public companies is spread through a large number of investors. Ownership shares can be bought or sold through financial markets.

Risk: The potential to gain or lose something. Throughout this book, we talked about risk in terms of financial risk (gaining or losing money).

Tax deduction: A way to reduce the amount of your income that you need to pay taxes on. If you pay tax on less of your earnings, you will not owe as much tax to the government.

Tax rate: The percent of income that is due to the government as taxes. If a person makes $100,000 in a given year and pays $20,000 in taxes, their tax rate is said to be 20%.

Easy Budgeting

Description		Monthly	Annual
Income: *How much do you make ?*			
Income	Income - "Take home pay"		
	Other income (after tax)		
	Total income		
Expenses: *How much do you spend ?*			
Financial Accounts	Student loan payment		
	Credit card payment		
	Savings contribution		
	Subtotal		
Living and Entertainment	Rent/mortgage		
	Utilities (electricity, water, gas)		
	Phone (cell / land line?)		
	Internet / cable TV		
	Home maintenance		
	Insurance (renter's / homeowner's)		
	Movies, etc.		
	Subtotal		
Food	Groceries		
	Dining out		
	Miscellaneous (coffee, etc.)		
	Subtotal		
Transportation	Car payment		
	Gas, parking, tolls, uber, etc.		
	Car insurance / registration		
	Car repairs & maintenance		
	Subtotal		
What's left over ?	**Total income**		
	Total expenses		
	Difference		

CPSIA information can be obtained
at www.ICGtesting.com
Printed in the USA
BVHW050955200619
551446BV00004B/61/P